Magda Hellinger was deported to Auschwitz on the second transport
from Slovakia in March 1942, at the age of twenty-five. She was one
of the very few to survive over three years in concentration camps.
During her time in Auschwitz-Birkenau she held various prisoner
functionary positions and had direct dealings with prominent SS
personnel, using her unique position to save hundreds of lives.

Maya Lee is the daughter of Magda Hellinger. She is an
accomplished businesswoman and fundraiser with several non-
profit organisations. After co-authoring an autobiography of her
Holocaust-survivor husband, Des Lee, Maya conducted wide-
ranging research to fill out her mother's story and *The Nazis
Knew My Name* is the result.

David Brewster is a Melbourne-based freelance writer whose
work is centred on helping memoirists tell their stories. David's
published works include *Scattered Pearls*, co-written with Sohila
Zanjani, and *Around the Grounds*, co-written with Peter Newlinds.

Praise for *The Nazis Knew My Name*

'For too long, the stories of people like Magda, who were forced to
make unthinkable choices, have remained untold. Unsentimental
and filled with detail of her courageous dealings with notorious
Nazis this is an important book that provides a rare insight into
everyday life in the hellish structure of concentration camps. This
thought-provoking book is a must-read for anyone interested in
the Holocaust.' **Ariana Neumann**

D0547599

The
Nazis
Knew
My Name

A remarkable story of survival
and courage in Auschwitz

MAGDA HELLINGER
& MAYA LEE

with David Brewster

GALLERY BOOKS UK

First published in Australia by Simon & Schuster (Australia) Pty Limited, 2021
First published in Great Britain by Gallery Books, an imprint of Simon & Schuster UK Ltd, 2021
This edition published in Great Britain by Gallery Books, an imprint of
Simon & Schuster UK Ltd, 2023

1 3 5 7 9 10 8 6 4 2

Simon & Schuster UK Ltd
1st Floor
222 Gray's Inn Road
London WC1X 8HB

www.simonandschuster.co.uk
www.simonandschuster.com.au
www.simonandschuster.co.in

Simon & Schuster Australia, Sydney
Simon & Schuster India, New Delhi

A CIP catalogue record for this book
is available from the British Library

Paperback ISBN: 978-1-3985-0629-9
eBook ISBN: 978-1-3985-0628-2

Typeset by Midland Typesetters, Australia
Printed and Bound in the UK using 100% Renewable
Electricity at CPI Group (UK) Ltd

In memory of my mother, Magda Hellinger Blau.
This is the story she always wanted to tell.

Contents

Introduction

Very few can understand what it was like to be a prisoner at Auschwitz–Birkenau – really only those who were there. Fewer still can understand what it was like to be forced into the role of 'prisoner functionary' within the concentration camp. To find yourself in a position in which, if you were brave and clever, you might be able to save a few lives . . . while being powerless to prevent the ongoing slaughter of most of those around you. To live with the constant awareness that at any moment, you could lose your own life to a bored or disgruntled guard who perceived that you were being too kind to a fellow prisoner, when all you were doing was trying to be humane.

My mother, Magda Hellinger Blau, was one such prisoner, though for most of her life few, including most of her family, knew her story.

Magda was always an enigma. Despite all she went through, she was not like so many other survivors of the Holocaust, who displayed the emotional scars of the experience for the rest of their lives. Magda was always forward-looking, positive and industrious. As my sister and I grew up, she would tell occasional stories of the concentration camps and her unique role within them in the same matter-of-fact way that another mother might tell stories of growing up on a farm. We had no idea. Eventually we would just roll our eyes and say, 'Just leave it alone, Mum.'

In the end, without telling any of us, she wrote and re-wrote her story by hand. She finally employed a young man to transcribe her words into a typed manuscript, and only then did we have the chance to read them. But Magda wasn't interested in feedback or clarification. In 2003, at the age of eighty-seven, she took the file to a printer and had it produced as a slim book. She organised a book launch to support a charity she was involved with and sold a number of copies. And that was that.

For the final years of her life, my mother wouldn't be drawn on her story or on the topic of the Holocaust at all. Though there was more of the story to tell, she'd had enough, and wanted to move past the nightmare of collecting her memories. It was as though the act of writing it down had cleared her mind of any deep, smouldering trauma. She reverted to the mother I had known previously – the one who only ever looked forward with purpose.

It was only after her death not long before her ninetieth birthday that I started to appreciate the complexity of my mother's story. In the late 1980s and early 1990s she had provided audio and video testimonies to the Yad Vashem Holocaust memorial in Israel, to the United States Holocaust Memorial Museum, to the Jewish Holocaust Centre in Melbourne and, a few years later, to the Shoah Foundation founded by movie director Steven Spielberg. She spent hours being interviewed for these projects but barely mentioned them to us. As I watched and listened to these recordings, it became clear that in her haste to get her story printed, my mother had omitted a lot of detail. She had also left out numerous primary sources that amplified her story, including the testimonies of some of the many women whose lives had been saved by Magda's careful manipulation of the Nazis. I realised that Magda had only told a fraction of her story in her own writings.

In the years since her death I've become increasingly committed to gaining a better understanding of what Magda and those around her went through. I've discovered a remarkable and unique story of a woman who had a rare, close-up perspective on the SS (the Nazis' elite paramilitary *Schutzstaffel*) and their murdering, lying and deceitful tricks, who somehow found the inner strength to rise above the cruelty and horror of the most notorious Nazi concentration camp, and who over three-and-a-half years was able to save not only herself, but also hundreds of others.

Little has been written about the people like Magda, who were prisoners themselves while also holding positions of responsibility, at the behest of the SS, over other prisoners: the so-called 'prisoner functionaries' of the concentration camps. What has been written tends to focus on the *Kapos*, who had particular responsibility over the *Kommandos* – the working groups who performed slave labour for the SS. Most of the *Kapos* were German prisoners, usually hardened criminals, who had a reputation for enormous cruelty. Unfortunately, this reputation meant other prisoner functionaries were tarred with the same brush. Magda has been misrepresented and judged unfairly by some survivors simply because of the positions she was forced to hold. Most of the accusations have relied on hearsay to denounce and condemn. In the early years after the Holocaust, Jewish survivors sought to challenge those who held such positions because they needed someone to blame. Many, including Magda, were accused of collaborating with the Nazis. This culture of finger pointing has caused most people who held functionary positions to maintain their silence to avoid prompting further accusations.

However, to judge Magda or any of the other functionaries is to ignore the fact that they put their lives at risk every time they took some action that saved another's life. Their stories need to be told.

Magda never sought thanks from those whose lives she saved – simply acknowledgement that she had done whatever she could in a truly horrific time. What she also wanted, as have so many other survivors, was to hold those who would deny the Holocaust to account. In her words, 'I have often wished for the chance to ask these people why they deny my suffering and discredit my life and that of millions of others. Did we not suffer enough that we should now have to listen to such denials?' She also, like so many others, wanted to ensure that the Holocaust could never be repeated.

I turn to you readers, parents, teachers, professors, scientists,
priests, rabbis. Educate the children and general public about
the horrors perpetrated on all nations, not only Jews, under the
Nazi regime . . . I cannot undo what was done to me and to

countless others. The torment and nightmares wake me up every night when I close my eyes. I want to tell my story so people like you might become determined to ensure that the roots of such evil are never again allowed the grounds on which to spread.

Magda originally wrote her story as she recalled it. In her mind she was clear about events; about how she dealt with the SS monsters and her fellow prisoners. In retelling her story and filling out a picture of life in Auschwitz–Birkenau during the years of her incarceration, I have attempted to remain as true to her memories as possible, while adding the detail necessary to provide an honest but thorough account. In addition to Magda's writing and her recorded testimonies, I have also drawn on the testimonies of other survivors who knew her and of others who held similar functionary positions, as well as on the work of various scholars. Where the 'truth' is unclear, as it so often is in stories like this, I allow Magda to tell her story as she always told it from her own memory. This is particularly the case in personal interactions: dialogue recreated in this book is as Magda wrote or narrated it in her own testimonies, edited only for clarity where necessary.

In closing this introduction, I would like to share the following extract from an open letter by Auschwitz survivor Dr Gisella Perl. The letter was published under the headline 'Magda, the Lagerälteste of C Lager' in the *Új Kelet* Hungarian-language newspaper in Tel Aviv on 28 July 1953. Dr Perl was a Romanian Jewish gynaecologist whose family was separated and deported to concentration camps in 1944; she later published her own account of the camps under the title *I Was a Doctor in Auschwitz.*

The letter was written soon after Dr Perl had reunited with Magda Hellinger by chance in Israel.

We have only been in Auschwitz–Birkenau for a few weeks.

I only guessed it then, but now I know for certain. We, numbered or not, degraded beings, human beasts – we had no idea, no understanding of what was happening around us. What was the truth? What was deception? Who is one to believe? Who is it who directs this hell? What rules and regulations govern the fate of each minute and hour?

We simply do not know. I did not know.

I have been a prisoner for six weeks. I stood barefoot in rags at the roll call and watched. I looked and observed. The camp had a few prisoners in charge and there was one called the Lagerälteste.

I started watching her. I saw her with the eyes of a doctor, a psychologist. Under the hard features – that hard face she forced upon herself – I saw the fear in her eyes, the trembling in her fingers and the terrified pulsation of the veins in her neck when the prisoners strode in front of an SS woman or an SS man.

'Who is she?' I asked.

One evening I went to see the Lagerälteste, *whose name was Magda.*

'Who are you?' she asked, 'and what do you want?'

'I am a physician. I would like to have a pair of shoes and to speak with you,' I said with trepidation and eyes averted.

'Come in, sit down. I'll organise you a pair of shoes but first we will talk because I can see I am dealing with an intelligent person.'

As Magda spoke she revealed the complex and devious laws of the hell of Auschwitz–Birkenau. She revealed to me the horrors of the gas chambers, the crematoria, the experimental Block 10, the horrors of the 'punishment' commando and of other institutions. Ten years later I do not think people could imagine that these things existed, though it was not so long ago. They could not have imagined that hundreds of Poles and millions of Jews were murdered in this sadistic manner.

Magda talked and whispered while her face changed from one minute to the next. Instead of the hard lines, her face filled with tear-filled furrows.

'They always select a few people from our group – quite at whim, without rhyme or reason – and place them in so-called leadership positions, to be the connecting link between the murderers and the victims. Why? What for? We do not know. We only know this, that we are responsible. We are responsible for everything the SS do not like. Believe me, it is very difficult.'

She continued speaking with her head bowed.

'You are a doctor. Look out! Do not forget you are a doctor. Look out and do not forget. Whatever the Germans say, it is a lie. There is always something evil behind it. Here are your shoes. Come along sometimes and let us discuss things. We can help a great deal.'

This was my first meeting with Magda. In this way she introduced me to the reality of the horror. I watched her for a year and felt sorry for her for a year. I went to her whenever there was trouble and she always helped me.

I knew it then and I know it now: it was a bitter fate to be Lagerälteste, *to hold together 30,000 to 40,000 human beings degraded to the level of animals, to keep them in order while at the same time carrying out the fiendish commands of the SS supervisors . . .*

. . . Our Lagerälteste, *our Magda, was a righteous person. She fought like a righteous person. I thank providence that our Magda was like that, someone who believed and had faith that some day we will become human again. Someone who, everywhere and at all times helped us with kindness, defended us and saved us – sometimes with harshness and sometimes smiling or frowning.*

I feel that with this testimony I am repaying a debt of gratitude in the name of very many prisoners – and not least in my own name – to whom Magda, the Lagerälteste *at Auschwitz– Birkenau had shown so much kindness.*

I hope Magda's story will provide inspiration to a world in which the best of the human spirit triumphs and survives under the most horrific, trying and inhuman conditions.

Maya Lee

PART ONE

MAGDA'S STORY

1

Origins

I sat in a large, mirror-black limousine. Alongside me was *SS-Hauptsturmführer* Josef Kramer, commandant of the Nazis' Auschwitz II–Birkenau concentration camp, wearing the imposing grey-green uniform of the SS, including a cap with the menacing *Totenkopf* (skull and crossbones) symbol on the band.

It was May 1944.

Kramer had only recently arrived at Birkenau, but his reputation had marched ahead of him – he was known as one of the most notorious commanders in the SS. He was a huge man, over six feet tall and with peculiarly enormous hands. Rumours were that he had killed more than one prisoner with those hands. Over the coming two months he would oversee the arrival of close to 430,000 Hungarian Jews, all transported in grossly overcrowded railway wagons. He would oversee the gassing to death, immediately after they arrived, of over three quarters of these people in the camp's killing factories. During this period the population of

Auschwitz would reach its peak, as would its rate of extermination. Of the close to one million victims of the Auschwitz camps during World War II, nearly half would die in this short period, under Kramer's command.

I was a prisoner. Somehow, I had already survived over two years as an inmate of the Auschwitz–Birkenau death camps. I had endured disease and starvation, cruel punishments and abuse. I had narrowly escaped being sent to the gas chambers at least three times. On my left forearm I was branded with the tattoo '2318', and this – *dreiundzwanzig achtzehn* in German – was my name to most of the SS guards. However, to Kramer and some of the other senior SS, I was one of very few prisoners who they called by name.

Kramer's car travelled a short distance to what would become known as *'C Lager'* – 'Camp C', officially sector B-IIc – a newly completed prison within the Birkenau complex. The car stopped at the camp's main gate and we got out. Stretching away in front of me, ringed by high, electrified fencing, lay two parallel rows of identical barrack-like timber buildings. Identical 'camps' sat on either side of this one. The repetition seemed endless, and sinister.

Kramer stared down at me. 'Here you will be *Lagerälteste*,' he said.

Lagerälteste. Camp elder. Camp 'supervisor'. The pinnacle of the bizarre hierarchy of so-called 'prisoner functionaries'. I had been chosen, without any say in the matter, to take charge of 30,000 newly arrived fellow female prisoners. It would be my job to coordinate food distribution and hygiene across this collection of thirty barracks. Each barrack could have been used to stable around forty horses comfortably, but now a thousand women would be crammed into each one. It would ultimately be my responsibility to ensure that all of these women emerged before dawn each morning, and again in the late afternoon, to stand in tidy ranks of five, sometimes for hours at a time, for regular *Zählappell*, roll calls. Any mishap, any misbehaviour, any failure of a prisoner to show for the roll call, and *Lagerführerin* (SS camp leader) Irma Grese or one of her guards would blame me. On a whim, a disgruntled or drunk SS officer could send me to the gas chambers. Any failure of hygiene, any outbreak of disease on my watch and I, along with all 30,000 inmates of Camp C, could be sent 'up the chimney'.

I took in the scene, squinting dispassionately through the persistent haze of acrid smoke originating from tall brick chimneys barely visible in the middle distance. Dispassionately? That was the emotion I allowed myself to show Kramer. Deep inside, I held back a storm of feelings, an amplified version of the same things I had felt every day for the past two years. Fear, the same as every prisoner lived with, all day, every day. Dread, for the lives, thousands of them, that I knew would be lost no matter what I did. And determination, to continue the mission I believed I had, to save as many lives as I could, regardless.

———

One of my earliest memories is of confronting a man in uniform. It is one of those memories I'm not sure is my own, as I was only three years old. Perhaps I only remember the story. I do remember the bright red dress that, with a three-year-old's stubbornness,

I refused to give up for any other clothes, all the time ignoring a commotion going on in the house next door. This would have been fine except that mixing Judaism with the colour red was dangerous at that time.

It was 1919, two years after revolutionary Bolshevik communists in Russia rose to power under their red flag. The newly established democracy of Czechoslovakia, born out of the post-war collapse of the Austro-Hungarian Empire, was one of the allied countries committed to overthrowing the Bolsheviks. As anti-communist sentiment grew, the hunt was on across much of Europe for those suspected of being communist sympathisers. A brewing conspiracy theory blaming Jews for starting the Russian Revolution made many Jewish people guilty of this 'crime'.

In our home town of Michalovce, at the eastern end of Czechoslovakia, rumours circulated that Jews would be executed as communists. A delegation of Jews from Michalovce approached our neighbour, prominent citizen Mr Elefant, pleading for safety. Mr Elefant agreed to hide them, but when word of his resistance reached high-ranking Czech officials he was ordered to surrender these Jews. After he refused, the officials burst into Mr Elefant's house, rounded up all who were hiding there, ordered them outside and stood them up against a wall to be shot.

In our house I maintained my own resistance and eventually, probably distracted by the noise next door, my mother gave in and let me put on my favourite dress. Moments later one of the Czech officials burst into our house, looking for more Jewish communists, and the first colour he would have seen was the bright red of my outfit. He was followed closely by Mr Elefant, who continued his pleas to save the Jews.

6

My eyes locked onto the shiny buttons and paraphernalia of the official's uniform. Feeling none of the fear in the room, I reached out with both arms and he obliged by picking me up. I chattered away while playing with his buttons and patting his serious face.

Mr Elefant and my mother watched in amazement. After some moments, the official patted my hand, put me down, said goodbye to Mr Elefant, then rounded up his colleagues and left.

'I'm so sorry Mr Elefant,' cried my mother. 'I didn't want her to wear the red dress but she had to have it.'

'It is okay,' said Mr Elefant. 'That child distracted the officer and saved the lives of these poor, terrified people.'

I had arrived as the second child and only daughter of Ignac and Berta Hellinger about three years earlier, on 19 August 1916.

My earliest memories of my mother are of a happy young woman who was always singing from the operas she had attended in Budapest as a child. We had a big garden that was always full of fruit and vegetables, and in summer she would wake up early to harvest potatoes, corn, tomatoes . . . whatever was in season. I would climb the fruit trees for the best fruit, sometimes finding breakfast in one tree, lunch in another and dinner in yet another. Mother was always cooking or baking her own bread and *challah*, a plaited bread made for Shabbat (the Sabbath). Thanks to the garden we always had plenty of food, and my mother was quick to share with any of our neighbours. If someone was in need, she would drop everything to help.

One day when I was still quite young, I was visiting the home of one of my friends when I noticed that the stove in their kitchen was cold and there was no cooking going on.

I told Mother about this when I got home, and she stopped her Shabbat preparations.

'Tomorrow is Shabbat and they won't have anything to eat,' my mother said. 'Let's take them food to cook.'

As we set off, she explained, 'Mrs Finfitter is a very nice woman, but she will be too proud to accept food. I'll go in and talk to her while you put the food in her kitchen.'

I felt a quiet pride as I placed a bag of chicken pieces, chicken fat and some sugar on the Finfitters' kitchen bench.

Another time a playmate told me her family was eating bread without butter and had no milk. Her father suffered from tuberculosis and only one of her older sisters worked. I ran home to my mother and told her this story and she sent me back with sugar, butter, milk and pieces of goose for a good soup.

In his mid-twenties, my father, one of ten in his family, changed his career from accountancy to teaching. He successfully applied for the position of Jewish history teacher in the town after the previous teacher had passed away. He then travelled widely to visit sacred sites and study Jewish history before returning home to Michalovce to take up his new position. Having established himself, he proposed to Berta Burger, then seventeen, soon afterwards. He originally did his teaching in the only Jewish school in Michalovce, but over the years, as the town grew and new sectarian state schools opened, he taught in them as well. He started teaching German too, because he knew the language well and it became a fashionable language to know. (He taught me German, though neither of us could ever have guessed how that would be useful to me later on.) And then he started teaching adults who couldn't read or write, his kindness and generosity helping to overcome the embarrassment they felt about their illiteracy. All this took up a lot of time, and he would often come home to eat in the evening and then go back to work.

Ignac was well regarded and well connected around Michalovce. He knew the mayor, Mr Alexa, personally and, although a religious Jew himself, he was often in contact with the leaders of the Greek Orthodox and Catholic churches in the town. All these prominent citizens agreed with the principle of freedom of religion, and that Jews and Christians should be able to live alongside each other in peace.

I had four brothers: Max was older than me and the others, Ernest, Eugene and Arthur, younger. Except for Arthur, I didn't have a lot to do with them most days, as they would leave home early each morning to go to *cheider* and learn Jewish history and religion before they went to school. My closest friend was Marta, an orphan about my age who lived with us. Marta lost her father in the Great War, and then her mother and grandmother both died of broken hearts. This left her elderly grandfather to care for her, but the task was too much for him, so my parents took her in. Marta and I grew up like sisters.

Apart from the seven of us and Marta, our home often accommodated school boarders who were unable to travel home on Friday before Shabbat. There was also a dressmaker from another village who lived with us during the week because it was not acceptable for a single girl to live alone in a strange town. This lady made many beautiful dresses for me and my mother. And then there were the extra guests at the table on Friday nights for Shabbat or for celebrations of Jewish holy days, whether friends or visitors from school or a family in need. Luckily we had plenty of space in our house, which my father built and then extended room by room over the years as the need arose. On Saturdays, we would visit the many members of the extended Hellinger family across Michalovce to wish them 'Shabbat Shalom'.

We lived in a very nice neighbourhood with many children, both Jewish and non-Jewish, and plenty of extended family nearby. The father of the non-Jewish girl who lived next door made a gate in the fence so that his daughter, Marta and I could run in and out of each other's gardens. With a group of other girls we always had some activity going on. We would make up plays, sing and dance or play games. Sometimes the boys would join in too.

I enjoyed school and did quite well. I found myself tutoring some of my classmates in the afternoon, one of whom was the son of the mayor. He wasn't a very dedicated student, but we did become good friends and I got him to concentrate a little better. One year the two of us prepared a speech as part of celebrations to mark the birthday of the well-liked Czech president Tomáš Garrigue Masaryk. The occasion was witnessed by the whole town, and the mayor was very proud to see his son in this position.

It was a full life, with the freedom that comes from growing up in a safe and abundant environment.

———

My father was proud of his Jewish heritage. Instead of traditional bedtime stories, he would tell me stories from Jewish history. This sowed in me the seeds of a passion for Zionism that was further encouraged when I was in my early teens and a Polish Hebrew teacher came to our school.

At that point I did not know any Hebrew and came home one day to tell my father, 'There was a very nice man and he taught us to say, "Lo sham".'

My father laughed, saying, 'I think you mean, *"Shalom"*.'

'Yes, yes,' I said. *'Shalom.'*

This teacher started some after-school activities like theatre and singing, and eventually introduced us to a *mo'adon*, a sort of Zionist youth club. I enjoyed this very much and soon became very involved. Not long afterwards my enthusiasm was recognised and I was put into the role of *menahélet*, meaning leader or organiser, for the small children. Now it was me telling these young children stories from Jewish history and sharing the idea that we Jews would one day have our own homeland. I eventually became *menahélet* for the older children, and then for the whole *mo'adon*.

I soon learned that when an organisation finds someone who is enthusiastic and capable, they are very willing to make full use of that person's skills and abilities. I became involved in the Zionist youth movement Hashomer Hatzair, which we referred to as the Jewish Scouts, and was busy helping them to support the Keren Hayesod and Keren Kayemeth LeIsrael organisations, which both raised funds to help Jews establish themselves in what later became Israel.

I became good at organising people, and had no shortage of *chutzpah* when it came to asking people much older than me for assistance. While still a teenager, I travelled to the town of Trenčín, nearly 400 kilometres away on the western side of Slovakia, to establish a branch of Hashomer Hatzair. There I met with three sympathetic local councillors. They weren't Jewish, so I just told them I was setting up a new scout movement for the community. I suggested a fundraising event at which a flag pole would be erected with markings showing different levels of donation. People would be given a gold nail and a tag with their name on it and, at the opening event, each person would signal their donation by hammering their nail at the relevant mark on the pole. The councillors were impressed with the idea and offered generous donations of their own. This was important, because then I could go to members of the local Jewish community and point out the donations these gentiles had made. Of course, they had to donate more than the non-Jews, so I got some even bigger contributions. I recruited a local sewing teacher to donate fabric to make a flag and she had her students embroider our emblem on it, and I also convinced the local metalsmith to create the nails. We held a big, successful flag-raising ceremony and the new scouting branch was born.

I also organised many Purim and Hanukkah parties and balls as fundraisers. At one ball, when I was perhaps sixteen or seventeen, a gentleman approached me and asked me to dance. I told him that I did not dance. This was partly true – Hashomer Hatzair didn't believe in dancing unless it was the *horah*, a Jewish version of the traditional eastern European dance in which everyone joins together in a large circle. This man went to the leader of the organisation that we were raising money for and said he would make a donation if I would dance with him. I still refused, saying I wouldn't dance with anybody. The price went higher and higher, until eventually the leader said, 'Look, he is donating so much if you dance with him. What will happen to you if you have just one dance?' And so I danced. It was an expensive dance for him!

When I was about seventeen I also went to *hakhshara*, or 'preparation', which was a training program for young Zionists. The aim was that we should learn the sort of manual skills that we would need in Palestine, especially in *kibbutzim*. I went to Bratislava, Slovakia's biggest city, and worked in a parquetry factory. It was owned by a Jewish fellow called Wolf, but for some reason I was the only Jewish worker there. I was bullied a bit in this place, initially because I wore nice clothes instead of working clothes like everyone else, but the bullying continued even after I began to wear working clothes. I found that by keeping to myself and working very hard – I always seemed to be running – I managed to get through it.

Just as many teenage girls do with their fathers, my father and I had many debates over these years. Ours were mostly about Zionism. In these times the traditional religious Yiddishe Gemeinde, or Yiddish congregation, saw the Zionist movement as pursuing a form of sectarian nationalism that had little to do with the Jewish faith. Nationalism across Europe had already caused the Great War and was brewing again. Although my father supported the Zionist cause, he felt it was also something to be wary of, perhaps not to be pursued with such fervour. I had obviously developed a different view. 'It is very important that we should work and organise and travel to Palestine and start there. When we get our new state, somebody needs to be there.' Our debates were intense and sometimes perhaps a little loud, but thankfully we were smart enough to respect each other's views in the end.

But Zionism wasn't enough for me to put my energy into. While on summer break when I was sixteen or seventeen, Marta and I decided that Michalovce needed a kindergarten to entertain the younger children during the long holidays. Of course, we didn't have any money or a place to set up our little business, so we approached a prominent local elderly woman known as Gleich Mamma. Gleich Mamma was the sort of person who made everyone's business her own, like an adopted aunt for children all over the town. She also had the connections to get things done. She told us she knew of someone who was getting married in three months, but in the meantime the new house they had bought was empty. It would be especially perfect because the garden had not yet been made, so we could easily create a sandpit.

The man who owned the house was a furniture maker, so Gleich Mamma asked him to make some small tables and chairs for us. And then, with her help, we approached local stores and managed to gather up donations of toys and books and rugs. We furnished the largest room as our kindergarten and were soon ready to go. We went around the town and told interested parents that we would collect their children in the morning and bring them home each night. To our delight, on our first morning about forty children were waiting outside their homes calling out, 'Malka, Jaffa' (our Hebrew names). Like pied pipers, we gathered our charges and marched them off to our new kindergarten. We continued to do this for the whole summer break, the parents paying a fee, whatever they could afford, that was enough to cover paying some rent, the cost of the sand and so on.

Through all of this, especially the Hashomer Hatzair activities, I relied a lot on my mother. In the early years when I was still quite young, she would drop me off and pick me up when I had meetings to attend. 'I don't think the government has so many meetings,' she used to say. 'You are so always so busy.' Once, when we were attending *kever avot*, an annual occasion when the wider family met at the gravesite of our ancestors for prayers, I overheard my mother complaining to her sister. She told her I was 'so busy with this and that, Keren Hayesod and Keren Kayemeth and everything. Whatever there is, she must be in it.'

My aunt replied, 'She can't help it. This is her mission in life. Didn't the Belzer rabbi say that she has a mission? So be patient. She is a clever girl, an outstanding girl doing many good things. So accept that. She can't help it. This is her fate.'

I didn't know what my aunt was talking about, but I was glad that she supported me. And the truth was that even if they weren't always willing supporters, my parents always went along with what I wanted to do.

————

During one of my organising trips with Hashomer Hatzair, to Kapušany, about an hour from Michalovce, I was billeted with the town's local doctor, Dr Tomashov, and his wife. He was quite a senior doctor with a big personality, and was well known for treating goitre, which was quite common at the time. I remember he had a typewriter that I used to type up lists and programs, and even the script for a play that a group of young children would perform.

A year later Dr Tomashov wrote to me asking if I would like to work with him and learn something about medicine, with the idea of eventually becoming his assistant so his wife could retire. For a long time I had liked the idea of being a doctor, and by then I was nineteen and looking for a career, so I accepted his offer and moved back to stay with him again. He sent me to spend time at the hospital so I would learn some of the basics, and I did his typing and learnt how to do things like bandaging wounds. It was a busy period. Dr Tomashov's wife went away for a while and, as we had no time to cook, we usually ate at a nearby restaurant.

One day I received a letter from a friend of mine back home. She said she had been hearing rumours from Gleich Mamma that the doctor had fallen in love with me, and that he wanted to divorce his wife and marry me. I was shocked by this. It seemed ridiculous, if only because he was so much older than me. In fact, it seemed so outrageous that I decided the best way to deal with the rumour was to just ask.

Over dinner at the restaurant that night, I told him about the letter and the gossip it contained. On hearing this, he dropped his cutlery and stared at me.

'I'm sorry,' I said, 'but I could never do that.'

Soon after, when his wife returned and could work as his assistant again, I left Dr Tomashov and returned home.

After this experience I had second thoughts about studying medicine. I thought about how long it would take to study, and also how costly it would be to set up a practice. Perhaps I should stick to kindergarten teaching, which I already knew I enjoyed and could do. Perhaps I could find a husband who was a doctor . . . but a little closer to my own age!

I enrolled to formally study kindergarten teaching in the town of Trebišov, 25 kilometres from Michalovce. At the age of twenty and with no other work, having left behind my youth work for Zionism, I devoted myself entirely to my study. I travelled to Bratislava to do my exams, and successfully finished the four-year course in just two years.

I returned home with the intention to set up a permanent kindergarten in Michalovce – the town's first.

Soon after returning I came across Mr Alexa, who was still our town's mayor, in the street one day and he asked where I had been for the past few years. I told him my plans and his eyes widened with enthusiasm.

'Magda, come with me.' He smiled. 'I have a house in Turecká Street that has some offices in the front, but the rest is empty.'

He took me to a neat house with a foyer and three adjoining rooms. It even had a small amount of furniture that would allow me to get started until I could afford some more.

'It's perfect. What's the rent?'

'Would I ask rent from you?' he said. Lighting a cigarette, he continued. 'You know, many years ago there was a kindergarten in Michalovce, and I think I might know where the furniture is. I'll organise to have it sent to your new kindergarten.'

I was speechless, but the mayor was insistent. 'You deserve it,' he said.

I was able to open the doors soon after, and within days my kindergarten was registered with the schools inspectorate and fully booked with children from both Jewish and non-Jewish families. I was soon in a routine, taking the short walk to work each morning, greeting Mr Kahot, the local shoemaker, along the way – a family man who had made me many pairs of beautiful boots – spending time with Marta and other friends on my weekends. As the calendar rolled into 1940, I felt that my life was set on course. I was proud to have taken charge of my own affairs and to have my own business.

———

In early 1942, a train conductor told someone, who told others, who told still others, that he had heard that young unmarried Jewish women were to be taken away to work in German factories. A shiver of panic and disbelief spread through our local Jewish community. The conductor, it was said, had sent his girlfriend away to the countryside to hide. I started to hear stories about other girls being sent away – one to Ireland, one to England, a few to Hungary.

Life had started to change for much of the Jewish population of Czechoslovakia towards the end of 1938, though I had hardly noticed. I lived in a very small world dominated by the day-to-day running of my kindergarten. In any case, it was some time before things would change for the 4000 Jews of Michalovce, in part because our region was in the far east of the country.

After its creation at the end of World War I, Czechoslovakia had become one of the few fully functioning democracies in central or eastern Europe. It stayed that way until Hitler started to forcefully expand his regime, rapidly taking control of the Czech half of the country in 1939. The Slovakia that remained soon became a puppet state of Nazi Germany with the help of the fascist and nationalistic Slovak People's Party and their SS-trained militia, the Hlinka Guard. A policy of 'Aryanisa-tion' was soon enacted, followed by the so-called 'Jewish Code'.

Most Jewish doctors and lawyers were forced to cease practicing. Eventually, 436 Jewish businesses were confiscated in Michalovce, along with dozens of properties. All were gifted to loyal members of the Slovak People's Party and the Hlinka Guard. Jews were displaced from their jobs, especially those working as public servants, and Jewish children were expelled from public schools. As in Germany, most Jews were ordered to wear a yellow Star of David.

My kindergarten was somehow allowed to continue operating, perhaps because it was authorised by the schools inspectorate, or because it was open to non-Jewish families; I never knew precisely why. I wasn't even required to wear the yellow star. The most obvious change was that fathers, not mothers, started to bring and pick up their children each day. Deprived of their livelihoods, perhaps this was their only way of maintaining a sense of purpose. We only asked for fees from those who could still afford to pay. Otherwise, life went on. In the evenings, if I had the energy, I would go to the cinema with friends – both Jewish and non-Jewish. If I gave the rumours any thought, I assumed that if something did happen my position as a kindergarten teacher would provide me with an exemption.

There had been some changes at home; only my youngest brother Arthur and I remained with my parents. My eldest brother Max had moved to Palestine in 1933, and Ernest and Eugene went away to join the Slovak partisans in their underground attempts to combat fascist rule.

In early 1942 I was busy organising a big puppet show with Marta and her husband to celebrate the Jewish festival Purim. We hoped that the show might lift everyone's spirits. There were scripts to write and rehearsals to run. I so clearly remember the laughter and cheers of the young children as they enjoyed the puppet show in early March. It filled our hearts with joy.

As my mother used to say, 'It is better that we do not know what lies around the corner.'

2

Deportation

March 1942

I didn't expect to see Mr Kahot, the local shoemaker, at my kinder-garten. But here he was, arriving unannounced one morning in late March 1942. He shook snow from his coat before asking if he could speak to me privately. It was very odd. I hardly knew this man except for being his customer and greeting him on my walk to and from work. I knew he was a family man and well regarded in our small community, but little else.

In the office he lowered his voice to barely more than a whisper.

'Soon they will be taking away the young, unmarried Jewish women. They will be taken to work in the Bata shoe factory, probably for many months. But I can help you.'

'What do you mean you can help me?'

'Choose one of your children. I will declare it's ours and I will protect you.'

I stared at him for some time.

'Why would you do that?' I asked eventually.

'I love you and I want to save you,' he said, though with little emotion.

I frowned.

'But you are a neighbour,' I replied. 'I know your wife. She works so hard to look after your three boys. Are you asking me to be your mistress?'

'Do I have to spell it out for you? I am going to do everything for you.'

I couldn't speak.

'I need to think,' I said finally. 'I will talk to you tomorrow.'

Walking home that afternoon through another heavy fall of snow, I mulled over Mr Kahot's bizarre proposition. I told my mother about it and she was dumbstruck. She had heard the rumours too, of course, but like me, she couldn't understand Mr Kahot's offer.

'What a cheek,' she said.

The next morning there were notices plastered onto walls all over Michalovce declaring that all unmarried Jewish women aged sixteen years or over were to report to the town hall that evening. People rushed between houses, hunched against the cold, wearing deep frowns. As parents dropped their children at the kindergarten the words that peppered everyone's conversations were 'girls' and 'deported' and 'Bata' and 'exemption' . . . and 'why?' My staff, who were mostly unmarried and mostly in the targeted age group, talked of nothing else.

The shoemaker returned early in the day.

'Thank you very much, Mr Kahot,' I said. 'You are very nice, and I know you mean well, but I can't do what you ask.

I believe I will have an exemption, but if I have to go to the Bata factory, I will go. It's no big deal for me.'

That afternoon, Jewish families were gathered in groups outside their houses, everyone trying to make sense of the decree. Our neighbour, who was involved in the regional government, said he would hide his daughter.

'I can hide Magda too,' he offered.

But when I went to see the hiding place, it was a tiny cupboard with hardly any room to even move, no window and no light. How long could I survive in there? It would feel like prison. I decided I would try my luck with the exemption.

A few hours later two officers of the Hlinka Guard came to our house asking for me. They told us they were instructed by Mr Kahot, who was the regional Guard leader. We'd had no idea he was even involved with them.

My mother rushed to the shoemaker's house to plead for help. She banged and banged on his door, calling, 'Mr Kahot, Mr Kahot,' but there was no answer.

I went with the guards to the town hall. Some other local girls had already been brought there, or had simply gone along on their own because that's what the notices told them to do. The group included many cousins from my extended Hellinger and Burger families, along with former school classmates. Many other local girls I thought might be there were not. Presumably they had either escaped or been well hidden. To one side of the hall was a group of fathers who were being interrogated because their daughters couldn't be found, some showing signs of having already been beaten. Other girls had come in from smaller villages around Michalovce. Some of these were also cousins, while others were peasants from poorer farming families. Eventually there were about 120 of us ranging in age from as young as sixteen to around twenty-five, like me, plus a few even older. Many of the girls in the room came from ultra-Orthodox *haredi* families and had little experience of the world beyond their own community. Outside the hall, and not allowed in, another group of fathers paced the dark like tigers, each pausing occasionally to try to identify their daughter or daughters amongst the throng.

An hour or so later, my father arrived at the hall with a suitcase. Somehow I was allowed to meet him at the door. I opened the case and could see that my mother had packed all my favourite dresses made by our boarder. There was also a new pair of shoes, and a feather down quilt, both of which I gave back to my father. 'I won't need them,' I said. 'Keep them for when I return.'

My father told me he would go to the schools inspectorate in the morning and demand exemption papers for me. As a teacher himself, he knew my work would be regarded as an essential service. He reassured me that I would be allowed to leave this place and go home – I just had to put up with this one long, freezing night of waiting.

The anxious murmur through the hall eventually died down as everyone ran out of ideas about what might be going to happen to us. As one of the older girls there, I decided to walk around and offer what reassurance I could. Amongst the group of women I found Ilonka, one of my young kindergarten helpers, looking pale and afraid; she clung to me like a child. I came across a group of about a dozen young girls who had been brought in from outlying villages. They were wearing the traditional dress of peasants, with head scarves tied under the chin and simply decorated pinafore dresses with full, layered skirts. I worried that they would be demeaned and discriminated against at the Bata factory, and decided something should be done. I retrieved my suitcase and carried it to them.

'Please, you must wear modern dresses,' I said.

I led the girls to the bathroom and urged each to choose a dress she liked. After a flurry of fabric and excited chatter, the village girls emerged with their peasant heritage now well disguised. A keen eye might have noticed that some of the dresses were over or undersized for their wearers, but this was only a minor flaw in my plan. I put aside my now-empty suitcase, leaving myself with only what I had on, including my coat, my boots, a little handbag and a muff.

Soon afterwards I was approached by a Czech gendarme – a local policeman who had been co-opted into the Hlinka Guard. He told me he recognised me as his station was not far from our home.

'Why did you do that?' he said. 'Why did you give away your dresses? I never saw anyone do something like that.'

'We are going to the Bata factory and I don't want these girls to stand out and be ostracised. And anyway, my father will get me an exemption.'

'How can you be so naive?' he said.

Early the next morning my father went to the schools inspectorate. He returned, his face dark, and spoke to me through a window.

'The clerk told me that the young religious instruction teacher from the Jewish school had already paid him 20,000 koruna to buy your papers for herself,' he said.

'What? But she is religious. She prays to God.'

My father told me the clerk had made him an offer. '"Times are changing, Mr Hellinger," he said to me. "If you bring me 20,000 koruna I'll send for the teacher to bring me back the exemption papers and return them to you." I don't have that much money. I'm so sorry.' His eyes were wet with tears.

'Don't worry,' I said. 'I will be alright. It's only the shoe factory.'

'They have torn from my garden my most precious flower,' I overheard him tell a friend as he turned away.

At that moment the Czech gendarme approached me again. 'I heard what happened and I want to help you. I have an uncle in the ministry and will ask this uncle to organise an exemption for you.'

Not comprehending why the gendarme felt the need to help, I thanked him but didn't give his offer another thought.

That afternoon, on 26 March 1942, all 120 of us who had been removed from our homes were to be taken by bus to the railway station. A crowd watched on as we left the town hall, walking across the snow-covered road to the buses. Mothers wailed as they recognised their daughters. When my mother saw me she broke from the group and ran to me. Her face creased with tears, she held my head between her hands.

'My dear daughter. I must tell you something. I don't think you remember this, but when you were a little girl of eight your father took you to the famous Belzer rabbi. The rabbi put his hands on your head to bless you and said, "This girl has a special mission in her life. She is going to save hundreds and hundreds of Jewish souls." Remember this. Remember this.'

We hugged and kissed until finally a guard pulled her away. 'Don't worry,' I said. 'You will hear from me soon.'

Forcing myself to stay composed, I climbed onto the bus. As we drove away I waved to my parents. It was the last time I would ever see them.

———

At the station we were put onto a commuter train to the town of Poprad, 150 kilometres west of Michalovce. On board, the collective mood once again swung between anticipation of adventure, urgent worry and subdued anticipation. The relative warmth and comfort of the train – warmer and more comfortable than our night in the hall had been – sent many to sleep for most of the two-hour journey. I kept thinking about my mother's words, about the rabbi's blessing, and tried to reassure myself.

When the train stopped, we disembarked into disorder. There were crowds of girls all around the station, all having been brought in from other villages and towns in eastern Slovakia. Girls sat on their suitcases in small groups or stood in crowds or wandered aimlessly, everyone doing what they could to keep the biting cold at bay. Everyone talked about where we were going next, rumours flaring and dying like embers. Members of the Hlinka Guard made sure no one was able to get away, but otherwise imposed no organisation at all.

Somehow, amongst all this, the Czech gendarme found me again.

'I have written to my uncle. You will stay in this place for two days and by then I will have exemption papers for you,' he said. He invited me to write a letter to my parents, promising it would be delivered. I wrote a few words on a page of his notepad – nothing more, I think, than reassurance that I was okay – and handed the pad back to him. Then he left.

Eventually we were all shuffled into a large building for another uncomfortable night. It was a two-storey building of empty, hard-floored rooms. There was nothing to make it habitable – no floor coverings, no heating, no organisation. We were hungry and thirsty but were offered nothing. The only girls who ate were those who'd saved something from the train journey. We huddled together in corners to keep ourselves warm, some girls crying quietly, others objecting loudly about the atrocious conditions we were expected to put up with. If we were going to provide the government with labour, why treat us so badly? No one was listening.

Like most, my own memories of that night are vague, lost in shock and the fog of history.

Not long after dawn, guards moved through the building, shouting instructions to gather our suitcases and go outside. It was almost a relief to be on the move again. The sooner we got to our destination the better – surely we would be given food and somewhere warm to stay? As we stood in a single, large group on the icy ground, it was easier to get a sense of how many of us there were – about ten times more than the 120 of us from Michalovce, I thought. A ring of guards stood around us in twos and threes, smoking and kicking at the dirty snow at their feet. Someone wearing a suit announced that we would soon be put on trains to Germany for work and that we would be taken home again after three months. His comments created a sprinkling of optimism through the group. It was short-lived.

After a while a train pulled into the station, but this time it was not a passenger train . . . it was a cattle train. No sooner did it stop than the guards around us became animated. They started shouting and pushing, herding us towards the train. Girls screamed and shouted as they tried not to lose their friends or family members. Ramps were dropped and we were made to climb up into the wagons, those with suitcases hauling them up as best they could. The wagons were featureless but for small, narrow, barred windows high up on the sides. Around ninety of us were squeezed into each, most remaining standing as there was no room for everyone to sit. There was a single bucket in one corner that we guessed was to act as the only toilet. Again, there was no food or water.

As the heavy doors slammed shut and were bolted from the outside, the gendarme and his promise blinked briefly in my mind. He had said we would stay in Poprad for two nights, but it had only been one. Whether he succeeded in his quest to get me an exemption I would never know, though I did learn sometime later that the letter I wrote was given to my parents and brought them some peace.

The atmosphere was stifling. We felt as if we were suffocating, there was so little air. It was dark too – so dark that we had trouble telling day from night. Initially things were quiet – fear has a particular smell, and a stillness – but before long a few girls started to panic. No one could quite understand why we had been packed into these cattle cars. No one knew how long we would be in them. Deep down, though, I think we all knew this train was not going to the Bata factory. As the world closed in around us, another thought returned to mind: my mother's story

29

about the Belzer rabbi. As I squinted through the gloom at the frightened faces around me, I wondered if she had understood the truth of the situation more clearly than most.

'If we keep together and help each other, it won't be so bad,' I said repeatedly. Drawing on all my kindergarten experience I moved to reassure one of the more distressed girls, then another, then another. But as the hours passed, the discomfort grew. The smell was terrible, the stress thickened and weeping turned to wailing.

Occasionally I asked some of the stronger girls to lift me up so I could see out the small openings at the top of the car. Mostly I saw just snow-covered farmland, but one time when the train was moving very slowly up a hill I saw a group of Jewish men working by the track.

I yelled out in Hebrew, *'Hem lokchim otanu. Ani lo yodaat le'an. Tishal.'* 'They are taking us. I don't know where. Find out!'

One of them waved to show that he had heard me.

Another time I looked outside after our train had stopped for a while. I could see we were in Žilina, a city in western Slovakia. As the girls lowered me down I announced that we were still in our own country, trying to convey a sense of hope.

Finally the train started moving again, now in the opposite direction but on a different track. When we stopped an hour or so later, the language outside had shifted. Looking through my tiny window, I could no longer tell exactly where we were, but I could see enough to know we were crossing the border into Poland. My grounds for optimism fell away.

'If we hold together we will be alright,' I reassured the others once more. But it was becoming harder to be heard.

———

We couldn't know this at the time, but we were being moved into Poland as currency. As part of an agreement between the Nazis and a compliant Slovak government, Slovakia would pay Germany 500 Reichsmark, plus transport costs, for each Jew deported for 'resettlement and retraining'. This was the Slovak People's Party's solution to their 'Jewish problem'. Jewish Slovakians would be providing much-needed labour to the Germans, but more importantly, the Germans had promised that any Jew deported from Slovakia would never return, and that any property confiscated by the Slovakian government could be kept by them. The welfare of people like us, their citizens, after we crossed the border into Poland was ultimately of little interest to the government in Bratislava.

Mine was the second transport of young women – the second thousand of 7000 women and 13,000 men who the Slovak government planned to deport in the first phase of this arrangement. Nearly 4000 women would be deported before the transportation of any men began. However, the Slovaks soon had difficulty finding enough 'young, fit' Jews to make up their quota, so by late April they started sending whole families away as well. In the period to October 1942, over 57,000 Slovakian Jews, about two-thirds of the Jewish population, would be deported to Poland.

Much later I would learn that my parents and youngest brother were deported to the Łuków area in eastern Poland in

May 1942. On account of his sound German language skills, my father worked in the post office of a small town for a short time. This gave him the opportunity to write postcards to my brothers Ernest and Eugene, and he had others from the town sign the cards so that their families might be reassured of their survival. On a postcard dated 28 May 1942, my father wrote that he didn't know how long they would remain in Łuków but that everyone was well and helping each other. He encouraged Eugene to go to the community office and ask for his (my father's) pension. It was not long after this that my parents and youngest brother were murdered, along with hundreds of other Jews who had been sent to this area.

———

'Raus! Raus! Raus! Los Los!' 'Out, out, out, go, go!'

We had little sense of time but it was late in the day when our train pulled to a stop. The doors opened to a scene we simply could not comprehend. Given the horrors we were to endure over the next three years – those of us lucky enough to survive at all – it seems almost mild in hindsight. But at the time, when we had expected to arrive at a factory, and not two days earlier had been sitting in the warmth of our living rooms with our families, this was too much for our minds to take in. So we didn't take it in – we reverted to almost animal instincts and did what we were told.

We squinted as our eyes adjusted to the light. The ground was white with snow, stretching to the horizon where it blended seamlessly with a pale grey sky. A rough path through the ice pointed to some sort of buildings in the distance. There were no platforms or ramps, so we tumbled out into the bitter fresh air. Without luggage I had more freedom to move, so after jumping to the ground I was able to help some of the other women down with their heavy suitcases, which they were then told to set aside. Uniformed guards snapped commands in German while dogs barked and snarled.

There are famous images of arrivals at the Auschwitz camps showing long rows of women and men, and SS guards of various rank chatting and smoking in small groups as they wait for the 'selection' process to start. This sense of relative order was not the scene in which I and the thousand or so other women of the second transport found ourselves on 28 March 1942. There was little of the renowned German efficiency on display. Our 'welcoming' party included a relatively small number of SS guards who had been relocated from the concentration camp at Ravensbrück in Germany, most of whom we would come to know as uneducated. They had been trained as brutal prison wardens, not as organisers or managers. There were also hundreds of female German criminals who had also been moved from Ravensbrück specifically to act as disciplinary support for the SS and to maintain order. Many of them took to their responsibilities with enthusiasm, yelling at and beating anyone who was too slow to disembark or to drop her bag or move away from the train. There was no selection – a sorting of who would live and who would die immediately. Selections on arrival wouldn't start for a few months. Instead, as a disordered group we were pushed and threatened down the pathway for several hundred metres until we came to the Auschwitz camp, stumbling under the now infamous *'Arbeit Macht Frei'* sign over the entrance.

3

Auschwitz

28 March 1942

We were herded into an empty, clay-floored building. With barely enough light to see, we could just make out each other's eyes and the tension and emotion in them. Shock, disbelief, incomprehension. And fear . . . fear above all else.

The group of us from Michalovce stayed together as well as we could. Some of the girls started to take off their heavy coats.

'Save your coats,' I said. 'Lie in your coat on the floor – it will be a mattress.'

Something about our welcome made me think we should hold on tight to anything we could.

And then . . . nothing. There didn't seem to be any guards around, though we were locked in, so we couldn't have gone anywhere anyway.

After an hour or two a group of the German women prisoners brought large kettles of tea into the building. As they put the pots down they said, 'Drink this if you want, but know that it is poisoned.' Then they left.

After two days of nothing to eat or drink, this was a cruel torture. But it didn't make sense. Why go to all the trouble of bringing us here to poison us on the first day? I thought they must be lying, so volunteered to take a sip of the tea. It tasted dreadful, little more than dirty water, but I didn't vomit or convulse. I tried some more and was still fine.

'We are all dehydrated,' I said to the girls around me. 'Take a sip, even if it does taste horrible.'

Later, the Germans returned with a kettle of lukewarm soup, telling us we should believe them that *this time* it really was poisoned. Once again I took the first taste. It was a putrid brew of rotting, fermented vegetables in dirty water and while it was even more revolting than the tea, and at first I couldn't keep it down, it wasn't poisoned. I held my nose and took another drink and this time I was not sick. I encouraged the others to have some, just to have something warm in their stomachs.

Now there was nothing to do but try to sleep. I lay on the dirt with my muff under my head, my coat's fur collar tight around my neck and my hands drawn up inside the sleeves. I closed my eyes and tried to make sense of what had happened to us since leaving home, and what might be to come. Around me, a thousand girls with a thousand emotions whispered, wept and slept.

———

It was not yet dawn when we were woken and ordered outside.

'*Zählappell!*' yelled the guards. '*Zählappell!*' It was a word we could come to know all too well. We were told to form five rows in front of the hall. The guards told us not to move, then disappeared, leaving us standing in silence. The chill air soon got through our coats, but no one dared move. We stood where we were for what seemed like hours.

As the sky brightened a little we could start to take in our environment. The place looked like an army barracks, with rows of brick buildings, two or three storeys high. Through a fence some distance away we could see other girls dressed in what looked like oversized and grimy old army uniforms, their heads crudely shaved. They were signalling us, though we didn't know why at first. Some seemed to be scratching themselves, others were pointing at their mouths or wrists or necks. They seemed quite mad, as though they were from an asylum. I thought that maybe they wanted food, but later we realised they were saying we should throw them our watches and jewellery, even our scarves. But why? And how long had they been here to already look so frightened and helpless? I would soon learn that these girls were also from Slovakia, and had arrived only two days before us on what would become known as the 'first transport'.

As time wore on a number of the girls around me could no longer cope with the cold. Exhausted, weak and terrified, they began fainting. I noticed a strong-looking girl who told me she was from Bratislava. As no one seemed to be watching, she and I carried the collapsed girls back into the hall and lay them down until they recovered.

Eventually more guards and German prisoners arrived. A leader barked that we should move.

'*Los, los, los!*'

Those who were slow to move were beaten with sticks until they did.

'Let's run,' I said to the girls around me. 'Let's be obedient and run. It might help us.'

We arrived at a building they called the 'sauna', where we were told to form rows again. Because I had decided to run, I found myself near the front as a group of us were told to go inside for processing.

No sooner did we enter the building than we were ordered by another group of female German prisoners to undress and throw our clothes on a pile on one side. For a moment I wondered how we would ever sort out whose was whose, but as I remembered the girls behind the fence I realised that we were probably not going to be getting our clothes back. We also had to remove any jewellery, watches, reading glasses – everything – and leave it on a table, again in one large pile. We stood naked and shivering, waiting for whatever was to come next. I looked around and took in the scared, humiliated faces, especially amongst the youngest girls and those from Orthodox families.

But the humiliation had only just begun.

In the next room was a group of men, each holding a large pair of scissors. We each had to stand in front of one of them. Chatting and laughing with each other as they worked, the men cut off the hair on our heads, as close to the skin as they could, then moved on to hack at the hair under our arms. Finally, as we stood on small stools, our pubic hair was removed. The men showed no care and their scissors were already blunt, so most of us were left with cuts and bruises. Still naked, we were pushed outside and across a courtyard to another building in which there were large tanks of murky chemical-smelling water. Ten at a time we were told to step down into one of these 'sanitisation' baths, the water freezing cold and deep enough to come up to our necks. Emerging from the bath, we were left soaking wet and naked until we went through to yet another room where we were each handed a pair of pants, a shirt, a pair of 'clogs' consisting of a flat wooden sole and single leather strap, and a wooden bowl and spoon. We were asked our names and given a yellow star and a piece of cloth with a number on it – 2318 in my case. The name and number were then recorded in a large book; the star and number were to be sewn to our shirt. I held my oversized pants up with one hand and my shirt closed with the other, neither having any buttons. As we stood outside, waiting for the girls behind us to be 'processed', we realised that our threadbare, filthy clothing bore the red star of the Soviet Red Army. These must have been the uniforms of prisoners of war. What had happened to those prisoners we couldn't know, but as most of the clothing was stained with dried blood . . . well, it wasn't hard to guess why their original owners no longer needed these clothes.

We soon learnt, too, why the women we had seen behind the fence earlier were scratching themselves: these uniforms were infested with lice. Lice that would now become our constant companions.

The last stage of registration didn't happen on this first day. I don't remember exactly when it did take place, but it was over the next few weeks. History tells us that at every other Nazi concentration camp, a serial number sewn to clothing was enough to identify a prisoner. But at Auschwitz a more permanent mark was required – a tattoo that would permanently brand us as Auschwitz inmates. And so, with a few scrapes of a needle into the skin on the outside of my left forearm, I became prisoner 2318 for life.

———

It was getting late in the day by the time everyone had been processed and we were marched to what would be our accommodation: Block 9. A brick building like all the others, it would house all 1000 of us, split across the two storeys. Girls pushed and shoved to get out of the cold, though it was not a lot warmer inside. With a few of the other girls from Michalovce, I found myself on the upper floor, where there were two large rooms crammed with three-tiered bunks, only narrow aisles between them. When I found a bed I felt the mattress, wondering if the handful of straw inside would hold any warmth or provide any comfort. But I was lucky, because when I put my hand inside the opening I found pieces of twine long enough to tie my shirt closed and hold up my pants.

As girls found places and reunited with friends and, sometimes, sisters and cousins, there was almost a sense of relief that perhaps we had finally arrived. At least there were beds. But looking around at the mess of us, at these bloody, scratched women all unrecognisable from just a few hours before, there was no talk now of factories or returning home. How could we know what was to come, when where we were now was unimaginable?

I noticed a woman with an upside-down red triangle on her uniform. This was different from the green triangles on the clothes of the German prisoners who had been helping the Nazis to process us. While she was shaved like us, so was obviously a prisoner, she did not seem inclined to match the brutality of the others we had come across. I approached her and asked her in German why she was here.

'I am Marie. I am the *Stubenälteste*, or 'room eldest', in charge of this room. But I am also a prisoner – a political prisoner,' she said. 'My husband is a famous Polish doctor and we live in Oświęcim, close to here. Before I was sent here, every day I could see through the fence that the prisoners were working very hard, and that they seemed to get thinner and thinner because they didn't have enough food. Whenever I got the chance, I would run to the fence and pass sandwiches through the wire. The prisoners would weep with gratitude. Then one day an SS officer approached me on the street. He beat me horribly then took me to his office, where I was beaten some more. They forced me into the camp and I have been here ever since. I have not been charged with any crime and my husband doesn't know where I am.'

As she spoke, two girls nearby started kicking and scratching, screaming and crying. Marie explained that it was common for prisoners to go crazy in here, and that if discovered they would probably be taken by the SS to the *Revier*, the hospital barrack, and given a fatal injection of phenol into the heart. I didn't want this to happen to these strong-looking young women. I believed they could be helped, that they were just in shock. I told Marie that I was a kindergarten teacher and perhaps I could help them, and she agreed. She told me she was a school teacher herself.

For the next few days I would sleep beside these poor girls, talking to them whenever I could. I patted their heads and faces, reassuring them that I was with them. After a few days they started to calm and were soon as normal as could be expected. They thanked me for saving their sanity.

None of us knew what was in store, but I realised then that my kindergarten training and youth leadership experience might serve me well in this place.

We saw no guards that night, and weren't given any food either. Next morning, Marie asked for volunteers to go and get soup from the kitchen building at the other end of the camp.

'Girls, we have to volunteer,' I said to the group from Michalovce. We had seen the kettles in the first hall, so I knew how big they were. I thought we would need perhaps four of us per kettle and sixty of us altogether, so I started rounding up a group of the stronger looking girls.

When we got to the kitchen we were the first ones there. The German women didn't want to give us anything at first.

'They told us you are prostitutes,' they said. 'You will be competition for us. It is better that you just die.'

'We are not prostitutes,' I said, noticing that they seemed shocked at my fluent German.

Another one looked us up and down and told us to show her our hands. 'You've never worked a day in your lives. How would you carry these heavy kettles anyway?'

'If we can carry a kettle, will you let us take it?' I said.

'If you can, but we don't think you'll be able to.'

'Let's do one better,' I said. 'Give me one of your girls, and if the two of us can carry a kettle back to Block 9, you will not bother all the girls to follow. You will just let them take the soup.'

One of the Germans, a well-built girl, volunteered. Between us we lifted the kettle of hot soup and started walking. It was heavy but manageable, so I thought I would raise the stakes.

'We will run, not walk,' I said. And so we did, taking the kettle all the way, then up the stairs of Block 9 without putting it down.

'You're a nice girl,' the German girl said after we laid it down. 'I like you.' She patted my hand.

———

Rumours spread early the next day that we were to be given work. Everyone started talking about what the jobs might be. Were we finally going to be doing some factory work? Were some jobs going to be easier than others?

One of the German prisoners came in and started gathering a group of girls together. She hauled them to their feet, telling them to go and wait downstairs. 'You will be doing agricultural work,' she said.

When I heard this I stood up and asked to join in. Outdoors, physical work must be better than being stuck in a factory. Better still, agricultural work would help me prepare for Palestine. But no sooner had I spoken up than Marie was in front of me. She slapped me across the face.

'I need this one here,' she said to the German. She pushed me back down onto the bed.

I stared at Marie after the German had left with the girls she wanted.

'She is a *Kapo*,' said Marie. 'The *Kapos* run their working *Kommandos* with brutality. And they are not doing gardening. They will probably carry large rocks back and forth to the screams of *"Los! Los!"* You wait and see how those girls come back this evening, bruised and exhausted.'

I listened in silence.

'Another *Kommando* is to demolish houses. I have seen this with the men. Do you know how? One group of girls will work on top of the building, the other group will work underneath. The girls on top throw the bricks down to the group below, who try to catch them. They often get hit by a brick, sometimes killed. If someone dares to say that they don't want to throw bricks down onto others, the *Kapo* changes their place and they work below. This is the Nazis' system. They want to dehumanise us, then kill us.'

Marie told me my job would be to help wash the floors and make the beds. And to bring the food.

'I will choose a few more girls to help you. You and the other girls will bring the tea and bread for the 600 girls in this section. If there's something to put on the bread, you'll bring that too. Later, you will bring the kettles of soup for the evening meal with the helpers I appoint. You'll be called *Stubendienst*, which means "room helper".'

That night, when the girls who had been sent to work outside returned as she had predicted, I understood that Marie was someone I could trust. They were exhausted and bruised, many with cuts.

'We just moved rocks from one place to another,' one said.

'We had to run all the time,' said another.

'Anyone who was too slow was beaten, and snarling dogs threatened us all the time.'

'We were demolishing a house so they can expand the camp.'

'We were dropping bricks onto those below us.'

A few had worked harvesting potatoes, which sounded a little less harsh, but for most their treatment had been brutal.

And it was only the first day.

———

With the arrival of our transport, and another transport due in only a day or two, the SS were struggling to organise themselves. We hardly saw any SS guards in the first day or so after we were processed. They left control with the *Stubenältesten* and *Kapos*.

Things changed on our third morning (or perhaps our fourth? – already time was becoming meaningless) when we were woken before light and rushed outside for the *Zählappell*. Female SS officers moved around our room screaming *'Raus! Raus!'* ('Out! Out!') They carried sticks, which they used to hit anyone who was too slow to move. Once outside in the bitter cold, wearing nothing but our threadbare shirts and pants and our open clogs, we had to line up in five rows as we had on the first morning. And then, once again, we were left standing for hours. Eventually two or three SS women arrived to take the roll – that is, to count how many of us there were and to reconcile that against their own lists. The uneducated SS women couldn't add up, and each mistake prolonged the whole process so it went on for hours. If a prisoner collapsed from standing so long in the cold, she was beaten until she stood up again.

These *Zählappelle* became routine, sometimes twice a day, taking longer and longer as more and more prisoners arrived and had to be counted. They would dominate our days, taking up many hours early, and then again late, when most of the girls were already exhausted from work. The roll calls were another in the long list of SS tactics designed to humiliate and dehumanise us.

Between roll calls, our routine was work and sleep. The girls working in the *Kommandos* left each morning to their punishing work. With the other women doing inside work, I went to retrieve tea for our breakfast, which we then had to divide between all the girls, making sure there was enough for everyone. We would straighten the beds and clean the floors then go back to the kitchen to fetch bread and, sometimes, margarine. There was never more than a small amount of bread for each person. Later, we returned to the kitchen to collect kettles of the barely edible soup. Again, we had to divide all this up between everyone.

It wasn't long before we started to understand how the systems worked and how we could use them to our advantage. I got to know a girl by the name of Katja Singer who had also been on the second transport and was now the *Stubendienst* of the downstairs of Block 9. Katja did not regard herself as Jewish, but had been living with a Jewish family in Bratislava and so had been caught up in the deportation. She was obviously a natural leader, and we soon became fond of each other and worked together when we could.

An advantage of the work we were doing was that we got to know other prisoners in positions that could be useful. I started making contact with girls who worked in the hospital barracks, requesting they bring me some supplies to help the prisoners who were coming back from outside work. We would use anything they managed to hide or make 'vanish'. In this way we were able to get some ointments for cuts and bruises, and sometimes medicine for diarrhoea. I approached girls who repaired linen and asked them to tear a sheet in strips that we could use for bandages. Over time, such activities would come to be known as 'organising'. Organising would play a vital role in all aspects of camp life.

I started to realise that, having avoided the outside work thanks to Marie's intervention, perhaps this was to be my job in this place: offering what help I could in the circumstances.

Each night when the girls from the *Kommandos* returned, we brought the kettles of soup upstairs. These girls were fed first, lining up silently – they had no energy to speak. One by one we would ladle out the soup, making sure to mix it well so that everyone got some of the few vegetables. After they had eaten, I used the basic medical skills I had learnt from my work with Dr Tomashov to perform some meagre first aid, applying the ointment and wrapping bleeding wounds or providing medicine if we had some.

One night a girl came up to me near the end of dinner time. She told me her name was Blumah and said, 'I am the daughter of the rabbi of Bratislava. He sent me to watch over you. You haven't had your own soup yet, so now you are going to eat or you won't have the strength to continue to help.' We became good friends, and also recognised a new lesson: that to survive this place we were going to have to look out for each other.

Unfortunately, no matter how much I or anyone else could do, the poor food and overwork caused many girls to become malnourished and very sick. Some died in their sleep. Others simply became overwhelmed by the misery of their situation. They would run from roll call and either be shot by an SS officer or, if no guards were around, throw themselves against the electric fences surrounding the camp, electrocuting themselves. Occasionally, from inside our block we could hear rounds of nearby gunfire, though we couldn't see them. These may have been behind the fates of those girls who simply disappeared without explanation.

Only a few weeks earlier, few of us had known death in our lives. Now it was becoming a frequent companion.

Some time after our arrival, Marie, who had continued to be as kind to us as she dared without incurring the wrath of the SS, came to speak to me, barely hiding a smile. She told me that Auschwitz would soon be liquidated and, as a result, she was to be given fresh clothes, released and sent home to her husband. All that was required was a medical check-up. I never saw her again. I would later learn that she was given a fatal injection of phenol into her heart. In the way of the Nazis, her husband would have received a certificate to say Marie had died of a heart attack. We would never know why Marie had been murdered, but perhaps she had crossed a line. Perhaps, in being kind to us rather than cruel, she had annoyed the SS who had put her in charge. Perhaps in that way her death was a warning.

For those of us who lived on, passing through summer and into early autumn, it became clear that the Hlinka Guards' promise that we would be returned home after three months was a lie. In the meantime, I made a decision to stay as positive as I could and to encourage those around me to work together.

The task of carrying food from the kitchen continued day after day. One time the German prostitute who had carried a kettle of soup with me on our first day took me to a room where there was salami, *shpek* (fat) and all sorts of other delicacies used for the senior SS. She said I could take whatever I wanted. I helped myself to smoked meat and a little salt, which I had been craving, but I thought taking too much would be dangerous. Then the woman started to become a little too friendly and I suddenly understood her interest. I chose my words carefully, explaining that I had nothing against her and that she was a nice person, but I was not interested.

Another time – it must have been around July 1942, near the end of our time at the Auschwitz main camp – one of the SS *Aufseherin*, female guards, standing around the *Brotkammer* (bakery) spoke to me.

'Wie heißen Sie?' said the guard. 'What is your name?'

I froze for a moment, surprised at her familiarity. But as we all saw each other day after day, some of the boundaries had started to break down a little. Perhaps she had noticed me speaking German to the kitchen workers. And perhaps, being quite young, just eighteen or nineteen, she was less clear about the rules than some of the older guards. She was quite wide-eyed, with a pretty, slightly chubby face and long plaits. She had only been here for a few days but I had noticed her because she was chatty with the other guards in the way of a young girl.

'My name is Magda,' I said.

'I am Irma,' she replied.

'Nice to know you,' I replied, as if meeting someone new at a tennis club, and before realising who I was actually speaking to.

Irma told me she had noticed that I carried as much bread as the other girls from my room, not leaving it to them to carry everything on their own as most of the other *Stubendienster* were doing.

'Magda, I respect you!' she said.

From that point on, when no one else was around, this guard always called me Magda and I called her Irma.

Occasionally over the next few days, Irma spoke to me again while I waited for bread. Sometimes she seemed to forget that I was a prisoner and she a guard, chatting to me as if to an older sister or cousin. She seemed to want me to like her. She even shared some of the Nazi plans that she had heard, including telling me that the SS were intending to use Jews as room and block leaders, instead of the German prisoners and other political prisoners who were currently doing those jobs. When I asked her why, she said it was thought these 'leaders' would become frustrated, angry and mean. This would create division within the Jewish prisoner population and these leaders would be blamed for camp cruelty, instead of the SS.

A week or so after this, Irma was no longer on duty at the *Brotkammer*. I would not see her again for some time. Little did I know that this young woman, Irma Grese, was destined to become one of the most infamous Auschwitz guards, known to many as 'the Hyena of Auschwitz'.

4

Birkenau

6 August 1942

In late July of 1942 we heard that we were to be moved to the new camp of Birkenau a few kilometres away. This caused a lift in the spirits of many of the girls. We had spent four months at Auschwitz in overcrowded accommodation, eating disgusting food barely nutritious enough to keep us alive. The physical demands on the girls forced to work in the outside *Kommandos* brought many to the edge of death.

Things had only become worse in July. For the first three months or so after the initial transports there were only young Slovakian women in our camp. We were kept in a section of ten blocks inside the Auschwitz facility, walled off from the rest of the camp, which was still occupied by male criminals and prisoners of war. Officially, we weren't even part of Auschwitz – our camp was an outpost of the main women's concentration camp at

Ravensbrück, and the camp commander and many of the guards had come from that prison.

Being contained to a relatively small area and all having similar backgrounds, we were, in a strange way, a community. We were even able to maintain the faint hope that we would eventually be returned home, as we had been promised.

Things started to change when more transports of Jewish women arrived from France and Holland. Our prison suddenly became much more crowded and stressful as its population doubled in a few weeks. We heard that a transport of families, including children, had been sent to gas chambers and murdered straight after they had arrived. This news sent a wave of fear through the camp population – not only for ourselves, but for the families we had left behind.

As our last hope started to fade, the idea of moving to a new camp seemed like it might provide some relief. How much worse than Auschwitz could it be?

How wrong we were.

———

When the day came to move, we were ordered outside for another roll call. We then marched for about an hour to the new camp. Some girls who couldn't walk or who struggled to walk were dragged aside by SS guards. We didn't know what happened to them, though rumours spread that they had been murdered.

When we arrived at Birkenau, any hopes that we were going to be better off quickly evaporated. What we found were rows of brick buildings that looked more like stables than accommodation for human beings. The barracks were surrounded by dark grey mud. Running through the mud, between the buildings, were deep channels with a layer of what looked like a watery sludge along the bottom; timber planks acted as 'bridges' over the channels. These channels were supposed to be drains until pipes could be installed, but we would soon discover that they acted more like moats than drains. Surrounding the whole facility, which we would come to know as sector B-Ia, was a high barbed-wire fence, and outside that were a number of watch towers. Across a road on one side was another fenced-off area that looked similar to ours, also with rows of barrack buildings. This was sector B-Ib. We could see that there were male prisoners there. And beyond the camp, as far as we could see, were hectares of desolate-looking farmland.

Before we were even inside a barrack, it was clear that while Auschwitz had been hell, this new camp was an entirely new form of damnation. Its heavy atmosphere seemed to shift the mood of the SS guards and their German prisoner accomplices. They were suddenly even more abrupt and cruel than before as they pushed us towards the buildings. I found myself inside Block 2, which was built just like a stable but where each stall, which would have been big enough to house a single horse, would be home to up to thirty women. Two crude platforms of loosely spaced planks had been constructed in each stall, creating three levels including the ground; up to ten women were to sleep on each level. Hundreds of women were to be squeezed into a single building. There were thin straw mats to lie on and a single threadbare blanket to share. The only light came from a number of small windows with no glass and from gaps where the sloping roof met the wall.

Those same gaps allowed any wind to blow through and chill us to the bones.

It was obvious that we had been moved to the Birkenau camp before it was ready for us. Unless, of course, the Nazis had no interest in our welfare, which was also becoming very apparent. We were no longer expendable prisoners who would provide free labour. We were now animals to be slaughtered at any opportunity. More word came back to us about people being murdered in gas chambers by the hundreds.

There were no toilets and no running water at the new camp. Our 'toilet' was a large hole in the ground with a plank over the top. It was bad enough coping with the stench of this open pit, but falling in became our greatest fear. Only a few days after we arrived, one girl lost her balance and found herself covered in excrement. She stumbled through the camp in search of somewhere to wash, but her effort was fruitless due to the lack of water. A guard chose the solution that was to become commonplace: he shot her dead.

The only water we had access to was from a filthy well with a bucket attached to a rope. When hundreds of women returned from doing outside work each day, desperately thirsty from having nothing to drink in the heat of late summer, they fell over each other trying to get to the well. Sometimes a girl would fall in and there was no way to get her out. Sadly, many drowned this way.

Even just moving around the camp was difficult. It was easy to get stuck in the mud, or to lose your clogs and be left without any shoes, or to fall into one of the channels and struggle to get out of the slush. While the open clogs provided no protection from the rain, losing them meant standing barefooted on the swampy ground. Worse, it became another reason for the SS to take exception to your appearance. Some women were shot on sight for the monstrous crime of having nothing on their feet.

One of the senior SS guards in the camp, whose name was Stiwitz, made a game of our wretched circumstances. At random, he would blow his whistle and shout *'Blocksperre!'* ('Lock down!') as a signal for everyone to return to their barracks immediately. In a deadly game of musical chairs, everyone rushed to get back to their block before the second whistle, girls shoving and falling over each other as they rushed across the planks over the channels. Many girls fell into a channel or became stuck in a boggy mess. Others were simply too weak to return in time. Those left outside on the second whistle were rounded up, forced into lines and loaded onto trucks destined for the gas chambers. One time I was outside when the first whistle blew and noticed friends from my home town fall into a channel. I ran to help them get out, but before any of us got back we heard the second whistle. Within minutes I, along with my friends, was being pushed up a ramp onto the back of a truck. No one spoke. We all knew where we were going. It was the first time I would find myself thinking, *Here goes my life, finished. At least I tried to help.* Moments later, just before they removed the ramp, a *Kommando* group marched past us, led by the same German woman who had carried the kettle of soup with me, and later shown me the kitchen store, back at Auschwitz. She was now wearing a *Kapo* armband. She noticed me and immediately ran up the ramp, pulling me out and slapping me on both sides of the face.

'I need this one,' she told the guards standing by the truck. 'She is part of my *Kommando*.'

She directed me to the front of her *Kommando*. We marched off, and as soon as we got around a corner out of sight she said, 'Go! Disappear!'

I thanked her as I ran away, still trying to comprehend what had happened. That night as I thought about how my life had been saved but those of the other girls had not, the Belzer rabbi's mission for me returned to my mind.

———

Katja Singer was appointed by the SS as *Blockälteste* for Block 2 at Birkenau. She gave me the job of *Stubendienst* for the block, so I returned to the same job as before: organising the cleaning of the barrack and the retrieval and distribution of food. It was different now, though. There were twice as many prisoners to carry food for, and there was none of the casual conversation that used to take place at the Auschwitz main camp.

I selected a team of sixteen helpers for the collection of the food, which involved carrying tea, soup and, at the end of the day, bread (400 loaves to feed 1000 women for supper and breakfast) from the *Brotkammer*. Many of the helpers had been working outside during the day and I knew they were exhausted. 'I know this is difficult,' I told them, 'but I cannot do this job by myself.' As before, I made sure to carry as much bread as they did. When we got back, we had to portion and distribute the bread, and any butter if we were given it. Mostly, if it was even possible, the food was worse than before. The bread seemed like it contained sawdust instead of flour, and it was always dry. But we made it go around. It was said that if you could survive three months on this food, you could survive as long as necessary. Unfortunately, many girls could not, especially many of the Slovakian girls who had arrived on the first four transports six months ago. Some would just die while at work or die in their sleep or collapse and die during roll call. Death was a constant.

As at Auschwitz, some structure and routine was established. It had to be – it was the only way we could survive. Wallowing in self-pity was an option, of course, but that wouldn't make the time go any faster or increase our chances of survival. We had to come to terms with this life, as much as it was a life, and navigate it as best we could. One day the war would be over and, if we made it that far, we could then return to our old lives, or at least create new ones. In the meantime, I repeated my mantra that if we stuck together and worked for each other, we increased our chances of living long enough to do that . . . though it was much harder now.

For a short time we were allowed to write postcards and letters to the outside world. Of course, they were censored, but a woman from Michalovce somehow worked out a way to carefully glue another card, or a piece of paper, over the top of the original. She would write what was really going on in Hebrew, cover the card, and then on the covering write in German the few words that we were allowed to write. Some of these cards were retrieved after the war, so we knew they got out. Some news about what was happening in the camps was getting out to Allied governments as early as 1942 . . . but of course nobody did anything about it. I sent some postcards this way to the brewery in Michalovce.

Not sure about the fate of my family, I assumed that the brewery was one business that would be allowed to continue operating no matter what, and I knew the director there, Philip Reich, and his wife Zelma, because their children had gone to my kindergarten. I sent a letter to them with the names of all the girls who were with me in the hope that they would be able to reassure their parents, and I did learn much later that those cards were circulated around town. By the end of the year the SS had either worked out what we were doing, or just decided that this one piece of humanity was one piece too many. Either way, there were fewer opportunities to write letters and cards from then on, particularly for Jewish prisoners.

The *Zählappelle* continued at Birkenau just as they had at Auschwitz, except that now they were more a matter of life and death. In the morning, often before dawn, many struggled to get up from their beds. The timber planks or dirt floor were so uncomfortable that sleep was nearly impossible. This, along with the pain many carried from outside work, and a lack of strength from the feeble diet, meant it was all some girls could do to get to their feet. Those of us with a little more strength helped where we could, but standing or kneeling – which we were often ordered to do – for hours in the cold early morning was torture. Then in the afternoon, not every day but often, we would have to do the same thing again, only now in the heat of the sun and after a day of work. We always tried to hold each other up, sometimes by linking arms along the row, but still some collapsed and were taken away.

———

Our camp became increasingly crowded as more and more transports arrived, some from Slovakia but also from across Europe. With everyone living so close together in the filthy environment, it wasn't surprising that disease soon took hold. Typhus and malaria both swept through the camps soon after we arrived, and the death rate rose quickly. One time I was walking through the camp and saw a big pile of naked bodies – girls who had obviously died of one of these diseases, if not of their work or starvation. Collecting them was the job of the *Leichenkommando*, the 'corpse unit'. It was such a sad sight – all these once beautiful young women. I went back to my block and told the girls that we needed to do everything we could to not end up on a pile like this. 'We must keep helping each other and encouraging each other.'

My turn with typhus came in the winter of 1942. By keeping Block 2 as clean as we could, we had somehow avoided the worst of the epidemic, but all at once around thirty of us came down with raging fevers and a complete loss of energy. This created a double threat. The disease was killing many on its own, but if Stiwitz found even one of us with the disease then our whole block could be sent to the gas chamber. This had already happened a number of times in October, when thousands of women were murdered in a single month. Everyone had to be at the roll call every time. Being sick in bed was not an excuse, it was a death sentence. For me, as *Stubendienst* for the block, my absence from any roll call would be immediately obvious, making my situation even more perilous. Worse still, we now had a German prisoner as *Blockälteste* because Katja had been appointed by the SS to the role of *Rapportschreiberin*, or record keeper, for the camp.

The German woman was not evil: she didn't expose my illness to Stiwitz. But she wouldn't go out of her way to protect me either.

My condition worsened. My temperature stayed high, and my tongue swelled so much I couldn't eat or drink. I couldn't see, couldn't hear, couldn't walk. I moved about by crawling along the floor, pulling one leg after the other like a little child, one of the girls kicking me to warn me if someone was coming. Standing in the roll call became impossible, even with the help of other girls to hold me up. Then a girl called Ruzenka had an idea to protect me. She asked another girl, who was working night shifts in the kitchen, to cover for me. She would say that I was doing the night shift, and was therefore sleeping during the day; in the meantime she would attend the daytime roll call in my place. When Stiwitz came into the block one morning and found me lying down, I somehow managed to explain myself clearly enough that he growled, *'Halt dienen Mund. Geh wieder schlafen'* – 'Hold your tongue. Go back to sleep'. Somehow this plan worked for me, even as, tragically, the other twenty-nine sufferers were sent to their deaths.

By that time, a few months into our time in Birkenau, some of the girls who worked in the kitchens or in the *Revier* (hospital barracks) had developed ways to 'organise' things that were needed. There was always medicine and food if you could find it – there was plenty on hand for the SS. It was even possible, with the right connections, to obtain items from Kanada, the nickname of the warehouse area where belongings that had been confiscated from new arrivals were sorted, mainly so that the Nazis could profit from them. The art of acquiring anything was in secreting a little away here and there, and smuggling it back to the barracks. This was incredibly dangerous – being discovered stealing could mean instant death. Luckily most of the SS guards weren't very smart, so the cleverer girls were very rarely caught. The ordinary SS guards could also be bribed with goods organised from Kanada, as they couldn't access these themselves. Clothes for their children were a popular form of contraband.

A request for medicine for me was passed to prisoners working in the *Revier*, but all they could access were some heart tablets. I took some of these but of course they didn't help my fever. Then girls in the kitchen managed to smuggle out some good soup with a few vegetables, which gave me a little strength. A little later I had a strange craving for tomatoes, an unheard-of luxury. But someone discovered that there were some prisoners who worked in a German research centre near the edge of Birkenau and that they grew tomatoes there. A girl risked her life to smuggle out a small number of these, and just the touch of the fruit to my swollen tongue was enough to provide me with some relief. Finally, as my fever heightened again, I deliriously asked for lemonade. This time it was another young girl from Michalovce who was able to help. She worked in the SS canteen and successfully stole some sparkling water for me. I think this brave effort alone might have been enough to save my life.

When the German *Blockälteste* started to lose patience with me and threatened to send me to the gas chambers, one of the girls told her she could sew very well and would make the woman anything she wanted if she could find some fabric. Another of the kitchen girls told her she was a good cook and promised to cook the German a nice meal. One after the other, the girls managed to buy me time and keep me out of the gas chambers.

One day in early 1943, in the depths of winter and before dawn, the SS guards announced that everyone – the entire women's camp – was to march outside the camp in ranks of five. No one knew why, but we did know that a reason wasn't needed. I still couldn't walk, so my friends improvised once more. I was positioned in the middle of a rank, and in the middle of a group, two strong girls on my left and another two on my right. These girls held me up by the elbows, my feet dangling below me, and miraculously my immobility was hidden amongst the whirl of all the other girls' marching legs. When we were told to stop marching, we found ourselves on a bare expanse of snow-covered ground. There was no work to do – it was just a form of cruel torture to leave us in the cold all day. The girls laid me down on a flat rock, moving me around and picking me up from time to time to prevent me from freezing. They gathered around me to keep me hidden from the few SS guards who stayed during the day.

Ruzenka had hidden a soup bowl under her dress, which concealed a bottle with tea. When possible, she gave me a sip. Other girls who were weak like me collapsed to the ground and could no longer move. If they were not dead, they were dying, and towards the end of the day the SS disposed of them like broken toys. As we marched back to the camp, the SS began pulling girls out of line who they thought were too weak to go on. Everyone was freezing, hungry and weak, but the cruelty of the SS had no limits. We would later discover that these girls – around a thousand of them – were sent to Block 25, the so-called 'block of death', from where they would all have been sent to the gas chamber. Once again, somehow I escaped this fate.

I finally recovered as the weather warmed up a little. By then, around a year after we had been deported, there were only a few hundred of the original Slovakian girls still with us. The typhus epidemic had killed many, as had the winter, especially for those who worked in the outside *Kommandos*. Those of us lucky enough to have survived this far were mostly girls who had the support of others, whether from their own home town – such as me and my friends and cousins from Michalovce – or from a particular religious group or youth movement like Hashomer Hatzair. Our survival was not in any way guaranteed, but if you didn't have others to look out for you, your chances were certainly reduced.

We fell into another period of 'routine'. The morning *Zählappell* started the day, followed by work, often another roll call and then what sleep we could get. In between, we ate our meagre rations.

On Sundays we didn't have to work and there were fewer SS around, which made for a strangely relaxed mood. One warm Sunday afternoon after roll call the SS guards left and we had an afternoon mostly to ourselves. I sat with a few friends, chatting and trying to ignore the incessant insects. As flies buzzed around us, driving us crazy, we waved our hands to swat them from our ears, noses and mouths. One of the girls said only the devil could devise something like those flies, which seemed to enjoy making a misery of these precious minutes of relative freedom.

Then one of the girls opened her pants and shirt. 'Let's distract ourselves by cracking lice,' she said, picking an insect off her skin and crushing it between two fingers. Lice were always with us, sometimes crawling under the skin and leaving infected, itchy welts. Just as often they were crawling all over us, including in

63

our hair. All these insects were constants in our lives and while they couldn't be completely ignored, we had no choice but to learn to live with them.

We joined in with the cracking of lice.

'Imagine doing this at home in normal times,' Edith said, 'lying about with our clothes half open, finding and squashing lice?'

We laughed until tears streamed from our eyes. It was these rare moments of tragic comedy that helped keep us sane.

———

And then I became sick again. I developed another strong fever, which was not another bout of typhus but another common disease at the time: malaria. This time some girls took me to the *Revier*. By now everyone knew that this 'hospital' was nothing like a real hospital, just a separate barrack with a few prisoners who were doctors and nurses who did the best they could with virtually no medicine or equipment. However, the girls thought I might get some rest there and at least be excused from the daily *Zählappell*.

I spent the night in the *Revier* listening to rats scurry about the room pushing or kicking them away when they tried to bite my fingers and toes. I'm sure they were succeeding with some other women who were unconscious or already dead. Rats were one form of torture that, somehow, did not exist in Block 2, so the next morning I asked to be sent back to my block. I would rather have died of my illness than been eaten alive by rodents. Later that day I heard that the whole *Revier* had been emptied, with all the remaining 'patients' sent to the gas chambers – something the SS liked to do whenever they decided the *Revier* was too full.

Once again I had somehow escaped another death sentence. Once again I was left thinking about the Belzer rabbi and the mission he believed I had.

5

Blockälteste

Early 1943

It was the strangest noise. It sounded like singing – I was sure it was singing – which was unusual enough in this place. Singing in any language other than German was forbidden, and as only a few of us knew German, well . . . most girls resorted to singing quietly to themselves, if they sang at all. But this sounded like a choir, and in full voice. It grew louder and we could see that it was coming from a group of women marching towards our camp. Finally we could make out the tune, and realised they were singing 'La Marseillaise', the French national anthem. SS guards ran alongside them, pointing their rifles at anyone who stared at the group and telling them to turn away.

No one who witnessed this scene would ever forget it.

They continued to march in time and sing loudly until they were inside sector B-Ia. There were around 300 of them, all wearing the upside-down red triangle badge of political prisoners.

Then Katja found me.

'Magda! I need you,' she said. 'I want you to be *Blockälteste* for these French women.'

'I don't want to be *Blockälteste*,' I said. 'As *Stubendienst* I am invisible. Why would I want to show myself to the SS?'

'They are French women who've come from Drancy,' said Katja. Drancy was an internment or holding prison north of Paris, from which prisoners were transported to the various concentration camps around Europe. 'These women are intellectuals. They are doctors, lawyers, writers. They need someone who can teach them how to survive in this place. Would you prefer I put one of the German prisoners in charge of them? They will likely be murdered within a week.'

She stared at me.

'You will take them,' she said.

'But I don't know French,' I said.

'Oh my God, Magda, you don't know French?' said Katja with a laugh. 'You went to school. I'm sure you know a few words. *Excuséz moi.* Something like that. The rest you will learn.'

She was right. I knew a little schoolgirl French. And now I had no more excuses – not that I had any say in the matter anyway. I would be in charge of these girls. I would be *Blockälteste* for the first time. I would be responsible for maintaining order in my block, including during roll calls, and for carrying out the instructions of the *Blockführer*, the SS guard in charge of each block (most often a male).

The women were moved into a barrack and I met them inside.

'Who here speaks German?' I asked.

A girl stepped forward, saying her name was Marie-Elise and that she was a journalist.

'Okay, I will need you to be my translator,' I said.

With Marie-Elise's help I told the girls, 'I didn't volunteer for this position. It's not a pleasure, but nothing in this place is a pleasure. With your help we can make all of our lives as easy as possible. We need to work together.'

I told them how typhus was raging in the camp, spread by flies and lice, and that it was very hard to keep the barracks clean but we had to do what we could. I explained how retrieving food from the kitchen worked, and about roll call. I emphasised that for roll calls they must be on time, stand straight and do as they were told. That way the *Zählappell* would not be any longer than it needed to be.

'Tomorrow morning we will wake up a little bit early before the roll call. We will do some exercises. Somehow we need to keep up our morale and what strength we can.'

I could tell they thought I was crazy, but they did it.

We could keep most of these girls doing inside jobs, saving them from the life-threatening demands of outside *Kommandos*, but it was impossible to save everyone.

Marie-Elise and I became a good team as she started to understand how camp life worked. One morning, a couple of weeks after the French women arrived, we stood ready for the *Zählappell*. An SS officer strode down the road towards our ranks and stopped in front of us. I stepped out and announced myself as the *Blockälteste*, recognising him as a doctor I had seen in the *Revier* once or twice. He asked me where the women were from and after I told him, he asked for a translator. Marie-Elise stepped forward and stood between me and the officer.

He told Marie-Elise to ask who could no longer endure the roll call. My heart sank. I knew he was carrying out an *ad hoc* selection. And I knew most of the girls, of course, were tired of standing motionless in the snow for hours every morning and many evenings, and that many of them would likely raise their hands. And I knew where the girls who raised their hands were destined to go. But what could I do to let them know?

After Marie-Elise asked the question a few girls raised their hands. I relaxed a little, as there were only a few of them. Unfortunately, it was not enough for this doctor.

He ordered Marie-Elise to ask if there were any others, anyone older or not feeling well who was finding the roll call too difficult.

As Marie-Elise translated this question, I elbowed her as firmly as I could without being obvious. Without missing a beat and without changing her expression, she completed the question then added, still in French, '. . . but it is better not to say so.'

With that, no more hands went up, and those that were already raised were lowered. Just one tiny older lady at the front kept her hand up.

Perhaps acknowledging that he had lost this game – for that is what such situations were for the SS: a game – the doctor started walking away. As he did so, the small lady started waving her hand, then called out in broken German, 'I am here, sir. I am sixty-seven years old and very tired.'

He turned around.

'*Kommen Sie,*' he snapped.

She followed him away, never to be seen again.

The rest of us remained in place and waited for the roll call.

———

After a year at Auschwitz and Birkenau, those of us who had survived the first transports were no longer thinking of when we might be returned to our families. We were now focused only on the basic instinct for survival. Any lingering hope that things might change evaporated with the sight of smoke rising in April of 1943 from a new chimney only 500 metres away.

It was always hard to know exactly what was going on outside our own prison, sector B-Ia, though there was never any shortage of gossip. What we would eventually know for sure was that the smoke was coming from a freshly commissioned gas chamber and crematorium, the latest initiative in the Nazis' efforts to streamline their mass murder. Over the coming six months, three more crematoria would start operating; historians record that at its peak this slaughter factory was able to destroy almost 5000 human beings every day.

For the rest of our time in Birkenau, the sight of smoke rising from these chimneys would be a ceaseless reminder of the Nazis' intentions for us all.

By now there was piped water into the camp and dedicated latrine buildings and washhouses. This was luxury compared with the holes in the ground that served as toilets when we first arrived at Birkenau, though the latrines were no more than medieval holes over open channels. There was still no toilet paper, and the ability to wash (without soap) was solely at the discretion of the *Blockführer*. There was no humanity in this 'improvement' to conditions, just an attempt to avoid another major disease outbreak.

Transports of new prisoners – men, women and children from all over Europe – continued to arrive almost every day, sometimes around a thousand people, sometimes just a hundred or so. Powerless, we would sometimes watch a stream of people, mainly older women and children, walking along the road in front of our camp to their fates in the gas chambers. Those women who were deemed capable of work were brought into our camp and processed much as we had been.

A group of Dutch women, genteel and refined young women, were not at all suited to working in an outside *Kommando*. The *Kapos* who supervised them were callous, and as the Dutch girls didn't understand them, they were often beaten for not following instructions. They were soon sent to Block 25, known as the 'block of death'. The SS used it as a sort of holding cell: rather than sending small groups to the gas chambers, they would wait until they had a large enough group to make it worthwhile. In the meantime, these poor souls would spend their last days locked up in that building.

The *Blockälteste*, a woman called Etta Wetzler, only made it harder for them with her loud and strict manner. Etta was the sort of *Blockälteste* whose reputation would tarnish all of us who held similar positions. Just as Irma Grese had told me would happen, by now there were many Jewish prisoners in these functionary positions. A small number, such as Etta, decided to ingratiate themselves with the SS, and did so by imitating the guards' brutish behaviour. This, too, had been the Nazis' intention.

In an attempt to offer these women some protection from Etta, Katja told me I needed to go to Block 25 to act as *Stubendienst*. Although I had the French women at the time, this move was not unusual. In her position as *Rapportschreiberin*, Katja did not formally make decisions about who would be *Blockälteste* or *Stubendienst*, but she had some influence over the SS through her close contact with them and in practice she made many appointments herself. She reported directly to the camp commander (*Schutzlagerführerin*, often known as just *Lagerführerin*) Maria Mandel. Katja had a very sharp mind and knew all of the movements in the camp. It soon seemed that Katja knew everything about who was who in Auschwitz and Birkenau. With her knowledge and contacts, she tried to ensure that mostly humane people were appointed to roles like *Blockälteste*, and she would often move *Blockältesten* and *Stubendienster* around where she saw an opportunity to make life a little easier for one group or another, or to provide them with some protection against a person like Etta.

The first thing I did in Block 25 was try to explain to some of these poor girls the routines of the camp, and what was expected of them. Even this small gesture earned Etta's wrath. She strode over to me and shouted, 'You talk to them like they are in kindergarten!'

Very soon these girls started to die. Some, starving, thirsty and exhausted, simply pointed to the heavens during roll call and collapsed dead on the spot. Within days, the SS decided that none of these girls were worth keeping. They were made to sit outside the barrack for a full day under a burning sun, unaware that they were waiting for trucks to take them to the gas chamber.

With another helper I found a bucket, filled it with water and took it to the girls with two cups, giving anyone who was able at least a small drink, or wetting their heads to cool them a little. Through the fear in their eyes I could see they were grateful for this small, if ultimately futile, mercy.

———

After another transport of Polish women arrived, Katja told me I would be their *Blockälteste*. I had two *Stubendienster* as assistants – their names were Stasa and Fela – along with a few *Läuferinnen* (runners). The runners were often younger Jewish girls, such as my cousin Aliska who was only fourteen years old. They would keep their eyes open around the camp and let me know what was happening. They could also deliver messages to or from other *Blockältesten* or the *Lagerälteste*, the 'camp elder', and would also come to find me if the *Blockführer* or another SS demanded to see me.

The Polish women who arrived at the camp were already diminished souls. They were survivors, having endured months in a ghetto before being transported like livestock. Then they had won the lottery on the ramp, at the selection immediately after arriving at Birkenau. They were sent right towards the camp rather than left, which would have meant immediate death in the gas chambers. But these women didn't look or feel like survivors when they came to us, with their hacked hair and ill-fitting 'uniforms', glazed eyes and drawn faces.

I spoke to the Poles in Slovak, our languages being similar enough that we could communicate. I explained the rules and routines of concentration camp life, which I'm sure to many of them must have felt cruel coming from another prisoner. Who was I to be telling them what to do? Of course, they did not experience the complete chaos that had greeted us on the early transports, when the only 'control' came from growling dogs and beatings by SS guards and sadistic German prisoners, but how could I explain that? Nor could they understand one of the most important things I had learnt: that maintaining order in our barrack helped avoid the attention of the guards, which was one way of staying alive.

A large number of these women were appointed to work with outside *Kommandos*. They worked on demolition of villages the Germans had taken over in order to expand the camp, or on extending Birkenau, or digging up potatoes, or on useless jobs carrying rocks from one place to another and back again. As it had been since the start, the work was brutal; most of the *Kapos* were still German prisoners given free rein to impose their cruelty. These women would return bruised and broken every night.

Sometimes as they returned they were ordered to stand outside their barrack for another selection. This was a separation of those deemed fit enough to go on from those too weak to work any longer. The latter would be sent to the gas chambers and 'up the chimney'. There was no pattern to selections – we never knew when they would happen. Sometimes they held them on Jewish holidays, as if to add an extra layer of cruelty. Sometimes they would happen if the SS expected a new transport and had to make room for the new arrivals. In their eyes none of us were any use unless we could work, and we were all destined to be murdered eventually anyway, so culling the camp of the weak was the easiest way to create space for an incoming group of prisoners who had not yet been starved and worked to near death.

The *Blockführer* had the power to play God on these occasions, deciding who would live and who would die. As the *Blockälteste*, I had to be there at every selection. It was the hardest thing. To watch, helpless, as one woman after another was pulled out of line, eyes wide with fear, and forced onto the back of a truck that would transport them to their deaths. 'This one stays. This one goes.' I was not to show any feelings at times like this. If I did, I might be seen as too sympathetic and sent up the chimney myself. As a *Blockälteste* all I could do, from time to time, was try to devise some sort of distraction or scheme to try to save a few souls.

If I had time before the *Blockführer* was ready to start the selection, I would arrange the girls in the lines so that the stronger, healthier girls were in the front and back rows and the weaker ones were in the middle. In this way the SS might not notice some of the weaker girls.

One time we had a different *Blockführer* who was a bit older. His manner was just a little less harsh than the typical SS guard, as if he didn't have to prove himself like the younger ones.

He turned to me and said with a half grin, 'You think I don't know you hide the weaker girls in the middle? I'll have to select them out of the middle.'

As was expected by the SS, I clicked my heels like a German soldier and announced my number. *'Dreiundzwanzig achtzehn.'* '2318.'

Doing this without hesitation was a simple way of making the SS think you were on their side.

'There is nothing wrong with those girls,' I said. 'They are not sick, they just need a little light work and I promise you they will be fine in a few days.'

'And what are they going to do?' asked the *Blockführer*.

Thinking quickly, I said, 'You see all those single clogs, the pieces of blanket and dirty uniforms all lying around? These girls can gather all of them together and wash them. They can hang the clothes to dry and pair the clogs so they will be reusable.'

'Where will you do it?' he asked.

'We will use the washhouse.' When he looked doubtful, I added, 'With this recycling we will be helping Germany.'

'And you want to organise this?' he asked.

'Yes, I will do it,' I said.

The *Blockführer* shook his head, though whether in amazement or amusement at this crazy scheme I wasn't sure. 'Do it,' he said.

With the help of some girls who were working in the storeroom we obtained some soap, rope and pieces of string. I organised for some extra bread and margarine to be acquired from the kitchen and took these struggling girls to the washhouse. The weather was kind for a few days, and with the lighter work and a little more food these girls slowly regained some strength. We took the cleaned blankets and clothes to the *Bekleidungskammer* (clothing store), ready to be reused.

I don't know where they got all the material, but soon afterwards these Polish girls made a beautiful 'pierrot' doll – a sort of clown doll with floppy long legs and arms, a round face and a pointed hat with a pom-pom on the end. The body was made from silk, the face white with beautifully painted eyes. They left the doll on my bed in gratitude for saving them. I thanked them with tears in my eyes. Even in this place and under these conditions, these girls had kept a sense of beauty.

But I couldn't keep the doll. What would I do with it?

I went to the *Blockführer* and asked, 'Are you married?'

'Yes,' he said. 'I will soon have a holiday and I am looking forward to seeing my wife.'

'We were thinking you should take her a gift,' I said, passing him the doll.

He was delighted, turning it over and over in his hands.

I wonder where that doll is now.

———

Being a *Blockälteste* was not a job you could turn down. If the SS decided you were going to take on this role, it was either say yes or go up the chimney. Katja's ability to influence these decisions had its limits. I decided that the best thing I could do as a *Blockälteste* was try to keep everyone working together and keep disease at bay. With thirty blocks in the camp, the less attention our block attracted, the less trouble we would get from the SS. There were exceptions of course, but many of the ordinary SS guards were bored a lot of the time, and also drunk, I suspect. They didn't give us trouble if we didn't give them trouble.

Of course, as a *Blockälteste* you were also looked at as a leader and counsellor at times. A girl came up to me one day speaking the sort of Slovak of the peasants. When I looked at her I realised she was very young. Another girl joined her who must have been her sister. They were blue eyed, with blonde wisps of hair starting to show on their heads. They told me they were from a small village in which they were the only Jewish family, which explained why they didn't look or sound Jewish.

'Tell me, Magda,' the first girl said in Yiddish, 'are we going to survive or are we not going to survive?'

'Yes, we will survive,' I said.

'But how do you know?'

'I know because they can't kill all of us, and those who work together will be the survivors. It's like Noah's Ark. You know that story?'

She nodded.

'By gathering some people and some animals and all working together, they lived on.'

She seemed a little relaxed by this story.

'You know Stasha, who we have been looking after in our barrack?' I said. 'She is not a Jew. She is a Polish prisoner, but she helped us, so we're helping her.'

Stasha was one of a number of women inmates who worked outside the fence harvesting potatoes, onions and so on. Sometimes they would throw a few vegetables against the fence while they worked, and in the evening when it became dark a smart girl would creep to the fence and tease these vegetables underneath with her fingers. This was one of the ways that we could organise a little more food, other than by having someone steal it from the kitchen supply. Stealing was very risky, though some of the girls became very skilled at it. I could never do this myself – if I tried I knew I would get caught.

'When I was taking some sick girls to the *Revier* one afternoon,' I told the Slovakian girl, 'I found Stasha sitting outside, hunched up like a little girl. "What happened to you?" I asked her, and she told me she had typhus and had been forced out of her block by the other women. I told her that she would come with me to our block and we would care for her. She would go back to her own block for the roll call, but stay with us the rest of the time. She looked after us, so we are looking after her. That is how we will survive.'

I like to think this young peasant girl had some hope after this conversation.

Stasha did recover, and she was so grateful she started to cry.

'When I was young, at my home and going to my church,' she said, 'the priest used to stir us up against the Jews, telling us that the Jews killed Jesus Christ and making up many lies. But my parents believed him so I believed him. There was a Jewish man near our house who had a long beard, and one day a group of us found matches and we tried to burn his beard. I am so ashamed about that now, after you, who are Jewish, saved me. If I survive this place I will tell the priest how wrong he was and tell anyone else that we should be friends with peace-loving Jewish people.'

Of course, not everyone did survive. But in my mind I always thought, you only go up the chimney once. Until you go, you have to do everything possible to avoid it.

———

It was a surprise to see Irma Grese again. I had not seen her since the Auschwitz main camp, but I came across her in Birkenau one day in April 1943. We were passing each other on the camp road, but it took me a few minutes to recognise her. She was no longer the round-faced, naive-looking young woman with long plaits. She was slimmer now, her hair pulled back tight under her cap. Her uniform looked smarter, better fitted, and her belt and boots were highly polished. There was a revolver on her belt and a whip tucked into a boot.

There was no one else around so I took the risk to speak to her out of turn.

'Irma, you look like a real SS woman now,' I said.

She didn't say anything for a moment and I wondered if I had spoken out of turn. Perhaps she didn't remember me? But then she said, 'Hello Magda.'

'I hope you never become as brutal as the others,' I said.

She looked at me without saying anything, then continued on her way.

————

As time went on, the girls who worked in the outside *Kommandos* became weaker and weaker. Even with any extra food we could obtain, there was never enough to keep them from fading away in front of our eyes. Many of these women soon succumbed to typhus and came down with diarrhoea.

This created a new problem.

It was too risky for women to go out to the latrine block at night. You could be shot for simply being outside. They had no choice but to stay where they were and soil themselves and their beds. How much of these girls' humanity had been stripped away from them! We had to do something. The stench was unbearable, and of course there was a huge risk of another typhus epidemic.

Birkenau was constantly a building site and scattered with discarded tools, offcuts and other rubbish. We just had to make the best of what we could find. Some girls found a few empty wooden boxes outside the hospital barrack, which they brought to the block. We made a hole in each box and placed them around the barrack with a container underneath, creating make-shift toilets where those in need could relieve themselves. An old wheelbarrow was recovered and positioned near the back door to empty these containers into; its contents could be disposed of at the latrine building the next day. But the problem still wasn't solved. The women on the top bunks were often too sick or too exhausted to make it down in time to use the boxes. While some relieved themselves where they lay, others used their eating dish to capture their excrement, which they then threw out a window. Much of it stuck to the window frame, and when the sun came up the next day and 'cooked' this mess, the smell became even more dreadful.

During a quieter time of the day when none of the guards were around, I began searching for a solution to this new challenge.

At the back of the camp I found a swampy area of mud that I thought was similar to that used by gypsies to cover the walls of their huts. Perhaps we could use this mud to cover the window frames? Better still, if I could organise some whitewash we could 'paint' the mud and make it easier to wipe off and keep clean.

There was a prisoner called Prince whose job was to drive a horse and buggy around the Birkenau complex delivering supplies to storerooms, kitchen barracks and so on. After checking that there were no SS around, I stopped him and asked if he knew where we could get some whitewash.

'We need two barrels,' I said.

'I know where I can find some,' he said, 'but what will I say if someone from the SS asks me about it?'

'You know they won't,' I said. 'You are just carrying out your orders. No one ever asks you. But if they do, just tell them it was one of the *Blockältesten*. Put the blame on me. I'll wait for you with a couple of strong girls and we'll take the barrels off your cart in just a few minutes. Please, we need your help.'

The next day Prince came past again, this time with my 'order' on the back of his cart. The girls hauled the barrels down and ran them into the barrack. Now to get on with our painting job.

Again when it was quiet enough we went 'shopping' around the camp. We found two ladders, some buckets and some long sticks and rags that could be adapted as paint brushes. Doing the job during the day would raise too many questions, so I decided we should do it after dark. Better to just do it and explain later. That night we went to work. We leaned the ladders against the outside wall and Stasa and Fela climbed up. They coated the bare timber windows with a layer of mud then whitewashed them, especially the sills and the wall under the sills. A few others painted the insides of the windows.

The next morning we admired our handiwork while waiting for the roll call. Our block clearly stood out as the cleanest in the camp with its bright, white window frames.

After roll call, Katja came running into the block.

'Magda, what did you do? They are going to shoot you or hang you. They're saying you painted the windows white to let the Allied pilots know there's a camp here. They're calling it sabotage.'

'I didn't know I was so clever,' I said.

'This isn't a joke. The *Lagerführerin* is discussing how to punish you. I'm very worried about you,' she said as she rushed out.

I went outside and there was the *Blockführer*, the same one I had given the doll to.

'I hear that they want to hang me for painting our windows,' I said. 'You should know I did this for hygienic reasons. You know typhus is raging badly and something needed to be done.'

He stared at me for a long moment.

'I did it for you too, you know,' I said.

'How do you mean?' he asked.

'The SS can catch typhus too.'

'That's true,' he said. 'Don't tell anybody, but I recently heard that 5000 SS men have died of typhus. A few months ago even a camp doctor died of the disease.'

My first thought when I heard this was *Good riddance to them,* but of course I kept that thought to myself.

The *Blockführer* told me he would explain my actions to the *Lagerführer* (camp commander) of the adjacent men's camp. And I had some luck. It happened that at the time the camp hierarchy were trying to find a way to eliminate the typhus epidemic and they saw sense in what I had done. I was taken in front of the *Lagerführer*, who gave me the authority to instruct the other *Blockältesten* in the women's camp to do the same thing. The *Blockältesten* thought my idea was crazy and were not happy to have me telling them what to do, but they had to do it anyway. 'Do it or not,' I said. 'I'm just bringing the message from the commander.'

Unfortunately, that wasn't the end of the matter. The *Lagerälteste* of sector B-Ia at the time was a Polish prisoner called

Stenja. She was very anti-Semitic and took personal offence that I had been 'promoted' over her head to organise this task. Stenja stirred up *Schutzlagerführerin* Maria Mandel and her assistant, *Rapportführerin* Margot Drechsler. There were always disagreements between the male and female SS officers. A female officer could never outrank a male, so women like Mandel often took a harder line to prove themselves. In this case, Mandel was affronted by her male counterpart giving orders to one of 'her' prisoners. She decided to take out her displeasure on me.

My punishment wasn't to be death (as it easily could have been), but it would be a whole new hell. I was to be the first *Blockälteste* of what would become known as the infamous Experimental Block 10.

6

Experimental Block 10

May 1943

'You are not Jewish.'

I was back at the main camp – Auschwitz I – and stood before *SS-Hauptsturmführer* (Captain) Dr Eduard Wirths, the chief physician of Auschwitz. He stared at my hair, which had grown back enough to show off its lighter colour and natural wave.

'*Dreiundzwanzig achtzehn* is reporting,' I announced, clicking my heels as I gave him my number. I looked him in the eyes – a risk, but one that I was willing to take. I would show no fear.

'You are not Jewish,' Dr Wirths said again. 'There must be a mistake. Your hair is light, and you are tall and slim. What is your name?'

'I am Magda Hellinger,' I said, wondering how I could be anything else but 'slim' in a concentration camp.

I chose my next words carefully.

'I am not Jewish? As far as I know I have always been Jewish.'

'What is your profession, Magda?' he asked.

'I am a kindergarten teacher.'

'See, I told you, you are not Jewish,' he said.

I had no idea what he meant by this.

We were upstairs inside Block 10, the block adjacent to Block 9, where my transport had been accommodated after arriving at Auschwitz the previous April. Dr Wirths told me this block was being converted into a special new clinic for health research, and that I would be the *Blockälteste*.

I looked around the dimly lit room, the same size as the space in Block 9 that had accommodated around 600 of us in closely spaced bunk beds. Here there were still bunks, but fewer of them – enough for about 400 girls in total – spread out a little so it looked more like a dormitory, though without any other furnishings.

I suddenly thought of testing whether Dr Wirths really believed I was not Jewish.

'If you want to make this into a hospital,' I said, 'I'll need sheets, blankets and pillows, and women's nighties.'

'You will have them,' said Dr Wirths.

Stifling my shock at this, I decided to see if I could push things further.

'I'll also need soap and towels.'

For a moment I thought I might have ventured too far, but he said he thought he could arrange these by the next day.

'And I'll need to bring a few girls from Birkenau to be my staff,' I dared.

He nodded without expression and left me there. It all seemed too good to be true, but time would tell.

I took some time now to look around the room again. Having the same layout as Block 9, it was familiar to me except that all the windows were boarded up with heavy timber shutters, only narrow gaps at the top allowing in a small amount of light. Otherwise, light was provided by weak electric lightbulbs. Were the windows blocked to prevent others seeing into our building, perhaps because Block 10 would now be the only female block on the Auschwitz I site? Or were they blocked to stop us seeing out?

The next day a group of young Greek Jewish girls from Thessaloniki were brought to the block. Their transport had only recently arrived and, having survived the selection, they had been through the sauna, had their hair cut off, been given old uniforms to wear and had numbers tattooed on their arms, much like us a year before. However, these girls received a pleasant surprise when they came upstairs to find their beds made and soap and towels waiting for them. After the nighties arrived, I handed them out randomly and asked the girls to put them on, no matter the size, and parade about. There was much giggling and laughter as the girls walked around the room, some short girls in nighties so long they had to hold them up like trains, while some of the taller girls were barely covered past their waists. There was more laughter as the girls clumsily swapped the nighties with each other until everyone had one of about the right size. It was a surreal moment of delight in this dark place.

———

Life in Block 10 was immediately different from Birkenau. Here, there were rarely outside *Zählappelle*; someone just came daily and counted the girls in the room. There was no going to the kitchen or the bakery either. Kettles of soup and tea were delivered to us by male prisoners, along with bread and margarine. And all in greater quantities than was normal in Birkenau. Occasionally the men in the kitchen even hid some salami and cheese in the delivery, or a letter or some sort of present. (One even sent me love letters!) There were proper toilets downstairs. There were hardly any SS guards around either – just two guarding the front door during the day. At night that door was locked and we were left alone.

This might sound like the place was luxury compared with Birkenau.

It was not.

Little daylight broke through the boarded-up windows, and the girls were never allowed to leave. Much worse, we would soon discover that the true purpose of the place involved torture, pain and misery.

Dr Wirths had told me this building would be some sort of research clinic, but it wasn't explained what that meant in any detail. The lower storey of the block was made up of a number of small rooms, some of them windowless, the others boarded up as upstairs. These rooms contained various types of medical equipment, much of which was still being set up when I arrived.

After the 'research' doctors came to start their work each morning, one of my jobs was to take girls downstairs to these men in the numbers they required. It might have been ten for Dr Clauberg, ten for Dr Schumann, five for Dr Wirths, and so on. Some doctors would specify which prisoners they wanted, while others were only interested in receiving a particular number of girls.

It was soon clear that the 'research' was neither innocent nor harmless. Some girls returned upstairs to us very sick. Some were vomiting, some had bad headaches and some were bleeding between their legs. Some did not return at all. I never knew the details of the testing that went on behind the heavy doors of the laboratory rooms, other than what I heard from some of the girls. Of those who were able to speak of their experiences, some told of stinging fluids being injected into their vaginas, which caused terrible pain. Some were subjected to some sort of radiation, to the point that they returned with burn marks on their skin. Others were anaesthetised so they didn't know what was done to them, but woke to great pain in their genitalia. Some discovered stitches around the vaginal opening.

We were able to get some other information from prisoner-nurses who assisted the doctors in their procedures, and who provided some basic post-operative care. I remember saying to a group of these prisoner-nurses at one time, 'Girls, we have to remember what we have witnessed here because after we survive this we have to be able to tell the horror stories. We can't write anything down, so let's put it in our mind to memorise everything.'

There were also prisoner-doctors who checked on their 'patients' from time to time. One prisoner-doctor who arrived at Block 10 early on was a French woman, psychiatrist Adélaïde Hautval. She was a tall, skinny Protestant woman who had been sent to Auschwitz for raising concerns about the treatment of Jewish women in a local prison. She had very straight black hair, which, because she was a non-Jew, had not been shaved off on arrival. In Block 10 she was ordered to assist Dr Wirths. Despite having no gynaecological or surgical experience, she had to perform examinations of the cervix and, sometimes, to remove parts of the inspected areas.

Adélaïde returned upstairs one night looking pale. She told me she knew the so-called research being conducted by Wirths was doing unnecessary damage to many of the women. She told me she could no longer do the work, that she was going to refuse.

'Do you know how you could be punished?' I said. 'They could execute you. Or you will be sent to an outside *Kommando*, which you will not survive long.'

'Whatever the punishment, I am still not going to do the experiments,' she said.

The next day she told Wirths that doing this work was against her religious convictions. Somehow she convinced him to let her stop doing the surgical work and, remarkably, she was not punished for her refusal. She spent some weeks assisting other doctors and caring for girls who had returned from experimentation, before eventually being transferred to Birkenau.

As prisoners it was always dangerous to send written messages to anyone. Should they be discovered, both sender and receiver could easily be sent to a *Kommando* or even up the chimney. For this reason, over time we developed a secret system, a grapevine, for passing verbal messages, using a chain of runners and other functionaries who had some freedom of movement around the camps. In this way, on this occasion, I was able to get an appeal to Katja for Adélaïde to be sent to work in the *Revier* instead of an outside *Kommando*. Not long afterwards, Adélaïde was transferred to Ravensbrück along with some other French women, which assisted her ultimate survival.

Another prominent prisoner-doctor was Dr Maximilian Samuel. He came to Block 10 a few months after I did. Dr Samuel was a German Jew who had been a prominent gynaecologist before the war. Samuel had fought for Germany in World War I, but that did not save him from being captured with his wife and daughter and transported to Auschwitz via Drancy. Samuel's wife and daughter were both separated from him at the selection on their arrival. His wife went straight to the gas chamber; his nineteen-year-old daughter was deemed able to work, but did not live for very long. Despite his age – he was almost sixty-two and quite frail at the time – Samuel was one of only twelve men on his transport to survive the initial selection. The SS wanted his medical expertise.

Initially Dr Samuel took over the work that Adélaïde had been doing. He often came upstairs to check on the women he had operated on, and because he was Jewish I was able to talk to him if there were no SS around. Dr Samuel told me he took orders from Dr Wirths and Dr Horst Schumann who, along with Dr Wirths and Dr Carl Clauberg, became the most notorious Nazi doctors in Block 10. He also told me that he didn't believe he would survive the camp because he knew too much for a Jew.

Over time it became clearer – and the historical records show – that most of the work performed by Clauberg and Schumann in Block 10 focused on different sterilisation techniques in an attempt to create an 'efficient' way of sterilising Jewish women as an additional contribution, along with mass slaughter, to wiping out the Jewish population.

As at Birkenau, I learnt to play different games, also dangerous, to try to reduce the harm done to girls. If some girls seemed to have had a harder time for a day or two, I would try to make sure they were allowed to rest. One time I asked Dr Samuel which experiments were the least dangerous. He told me that Clauberg's sterilisations were less likely to succeed. It was later known that Clauberg's work involved trying to inflame the Fallopian tubes to prevent pregnancy, whereas Schumann's work relied on the application of dangerous radiation to the reproductive organs. Clauberg's experiments did a lot of harm and succeeded in sterilising many women; however, many more of Schumann's subjects died. Many others were so badly burned that they were of no more use to him, so were sent straight to the gas chambers.

Dr Wladislaw Dering, a Catholic Polish political prisoner, was another prisoner-doctor during the time I was in Block 10. There was constant, obvious rivalry between all the doctors, both Nazis and prisoner-doctors, and Samuel would tell me stories about how Dering would perform surgery, including the removal of ovaries for testing, without using general anaesthetics or other medication, and would even reuse surgical equipment from one procedure to the next without cleaning, let alone sterilisation. Not being in the rooms, I couldn't be sure of the truth of these stories, but Dering certainly came across as sadistic, having little care for the women he operated on.

Jewish prisoner-doctors, in particular, trod the same fine line that other prisoner functionaries did, including people like myself and Katja. Our positions gave us a small degree of freedom and some opportunities, but we were expected to obey the orders of the SS without question. At the same time, many of us looked for opportunities to minimise harm and save lives if we could by taking advantage of our relative freedom, learning to understand the devious minds of the SS and the games they liked to play. The risk, of course, was that if we overstepped the line, if we were seen as too soft or not willing to meet the needs of the SS, we could be sent up the chimney without warning. In November 1943, when I was no longer in Block 10, this was the fate of Dr Samuel. I heard that he was removed from Block 10 one morning and never returned. Some women who had been operated on by Dr Samuel believed he may have sabotaged the work he was doing, by either going too slowly or not performing the procedures properly. It could also have been that, as he had told me himself, he simply knew too much about what the Nazi doctors were doing. The precise details of his disappearance have never been revealed, but it is almost certain that his execution was ordered by Dr Wirths.

———

One of the small freedoms I had as *Blockälteste* of Block 10 was that I could go outside from time to time, something none of the girls kept for the experiments were allowed to do. They saw no daylight except that which crept through gaps in the window shutters. One Sunday when Wirths was talking to me, I decided to try my luck with him once more. I pointed out that the girls had not seen any sun. Could I take them outside to get some fresh air?

'Okay Magda, if you must,' he said. I kept my surprise to myself.

It was a perfect day – the sort of day that could help us forget where we were for a moment. The girls harvested what small flowers they could find in cracks along the road, and one girl was even able to identify some wild herbs that we could later add to our soup. It was amazing how this hour or so lifted our spirits.

Another time I was on my own and walked along the road outside Block 10. I passed the brick wall that screened the court-yard between Blocks 10 and 11. We had often heard noises that sounded like gunshots coming from this direction, but we couldn't see out the windows so we couldn't be sure. It wasn't until after the war that the purpose of this courtyard as an execu-tion yard, the site of hundreds of murders, was fully revealed.

Looking through the iron gate in the wall and into the court-yard, I froze.

Lying together on the ground were the naked corpses of three young women. I recognised one face and realised they were three sisters who had not returned from being sent for experimenta-tion the day before.

I was overwhelmed by a sudden sadness and almost broke down. All this time, despite all the atrocities, all the death, all the sadistic abuse going on around me, I had managed to remain stoic even when my heart was bleeding. I was deter-mined never to show any weakness or fear to the SS. I was determined always to present a brave face to the other girls. But here, on my own for the briefest time, the bodies of these three healthy girls left out to rot like discarded carcasses . . . it shook me to my core.

———

Strangely, it was in the darkness that we found a glimmer of light.

The nights in Block 10 were a time of relative peace. At six o'clock each night, the doors to the building were locked and the SS guards went to their own barracks, leaving us alone. This, along with the blocked windows, which kept any noise from finding its way outside, created a rare opportunity for us to entertain ourselves.

Mila Potashinski was a famous actress, dancer and singer who worked as one of the prisoner-nurses. When I learnt about her skills it gave me an idea. She agreed to create a cabaret group, chose some of the girls and taught them to sing and dance.

After Alma Rosé arrived, these cabarets became much more sophisticated.

Alma arrived at Auschwitz from France on the 57th transport in mid-July 1943. Of the 1000 men and women on the train, she was selected with eleven other women, processed and sent straight to Block 10. One of the prisoner-nurses recognised her and pointed her out to me, saying she was a famous Viennese violinist. I didn't recognise her name, but when the nurse told me Alma had been married to Váša Príhoda, one of the most famous Czech musicians in Europe at the time, I took notice.

Here was an opportunity. I didn't yet know how it would help, but if I could organise a violin for Alma, perhaps she could be saved from experimentation. At the very least, her playing was likely to lift the spirits of the women in Block 10.

Using the underground messaging system, I passed a request on to Helen 'Zippy' Spitzer, who assisted Katja in the administration office. Zippy was a musician herself, so she understood the importance of my request. Between Zippy, Katja and a network of connected prisoners who worked in Kanada, a nice instrument, most likely confiscated from some poor new arrival, was obtained.

It gave me a lot of satisfaction to pass the violin to Alma.

That night was as close to magic as we were ever going to find in this place.

Once the SS guards had locked us in and left, I sent two young girls down to stand near the door in case anyone approached. Alma picked up her instrument, tuned it and started to play. What she played I do not remember, but in that grey world in which even birdsong was non-existent, we were momentarily returned to our old lives.

From that night on, Alma's music became a constant. She joined with Mila, who sang or recited poetry. With the violin, Mila's cabaret shows became more animated.

Over time, a full production was developed that was repeated time after time until, inevitably – probably from one of the prisoner-nurses talking to a doctor – word got out to the SS. But rather than resulting in punishment, we now found ourselves performing the show in front of a group of SS officers. It seemed that they, too, missed culture.

In the end Maria Mandel, after hearing Alma play, had her transferred to Birkenau, where she wanted her to lead an orchestra of female prisoners to rival an existing orchestra in the men's camp. Alma would lead the women's orchestra through the winter of 1943–44 until she became ill in late March 1944. Despite the care of the SS doctors, no doubt provided at the behest of Mandel, Alma died in early April. Mila would go on to survive the war, as did her husband Moshe. They moved to Australia and established a Yiddish theatre in Melbourne.

Block 10 has gone down in history as one of the cruellest places in Auschwitz–Birkenau. Despite that, our humanity was never beaten, and music had a lot to do with that.

————

There was another doctor in Block 10 who conducted anthropological experiments on women by making plaster casts of girls' heads. He told me he was trying to prove that the Jewish brain was smaller, and therefore inferior, to the German brain.

'There are fewer molecules in the heads of the Jewish person than the German,' he said.

He asked me to send thirty girls to the main *Revier* building on the Auschwitz site so that he could make plaster casts.

I joked, 'I want a cast too.'

'Sure, I'll make a cast of you, to prove that your brain is also less developed,' he teased.

A week later I was told to put those same thirty women into a separate room in the evening and to close and lock the door. The doctor left me with the key. At midnight they were to be taken by train to another town where the study on their brains could be continued in a sanatorium. Sometime after dark I heard knocking on the small metal shutter in the room's door. I opened the shutter and there was Mila.

'Magda, if they want to study our brains, they'll have to kill us first. Please let me out.'

I let her out, and soon after released another girl who pleaded that she wanted to stay with her sister. The SS were often disorganised, so I thought they might not notice they were two short.

Unfortunately I was wrong.

The two girls were missed, and the attention of the SS turned to me as the only person who could have released them.

'They're going to kill you,' someone said the next morning, and word spread quickly that I was to be executed.

I remembered what I had thought the first time I was in this situation: *Here goes my life, finished. At least I tried to help.* I wondered how they would do it. Shot in the courtyard where I had seen the three girls' bodies? Hanged in the open in front of the other prisoners? Injected with phenol? Sent to the gas chamber?

I kept doing my work. What else could I do? In the meantime, the Greek girls prayed for me.

A message came from Yaco, the executioner. Everyone knew Yaco; he was such a large, strong man that he seemed like a giant in this place. A Polish Jew, he had been a wrestler before the war. And he was strangely gentle, for an executioner.

'If I can't help you any other way, I will make sure it is quick,' was his message.

Somehow the Greek girls secretly made two beautiful pillows for me, which they left on my bed. The pillows were very soft and luxurious, but like the pierrot doll the Poles had made me, what could I do with them? It happened that Wirths' car was parked at the door of Block 10, empty but with the windows open. I saw his gun in its holster lying on the back seat. I ran back upstairs, retrieved the pillows, went back down and threw them into the car when no one was looking.

Soon after, Wirths found me in the hallway.

'I hear you are in trouble, Magda. Why did you release the women?' he said.

'I did only what I thought was right,' I said. 'I don't feel I did anything wrong.'

'Well, we will see. You will be called before *Schutzhaftlager-führer* (camp operations director) Aumeier.'

A Slovakian girl who worked in the administration area was sent to bring me to Aumeier. On the way there, she said, 'I am very sorry, Magda. Nobody comes out alive from this. Aumeier is a small man. But he has a complex, is strong and has murdered many.'

'I will say goodbye to you here,' she said as she pointed me to Aumeier's office.

I stood in front of Hans Aumeier. I had not seen this SS commander before but, as the girl had told me, he was a short, stocky man. He had a wide head but a small face, his eyes closely spaced and mean.

'Why did you release the women?' he said.

I repeated what I had said to Dr Wirths, that I did only what I thought was right.

He asked me the question again and I repeated my answer.

'Get out,' he said.

I turned and left, not sure what had just happened.

I returned to Block 10, where I was greeted with looks of shock from everyone who saw me. Everyone except Dr Wirths.

'Thank you for the pillows,' he said.

I did not reply.

And now the situation was repeated. Once again Mandel, who was ultimately in charge of Block 10 as a women's block, was unhappy that one of the male commanders had set me free, so once again she decided I needed to be punished.

It was Irma Grese who came to collect me that evening. I had not seen her since we met on the road back at Birkenau. She told me to follow her, without saying where we were going. Once we were outside and alone she made small talk as we walked, as if we were back at the bakery where we had first met. She said nothing about my supposed 'crime'. It seems surreal to think about now. I only half listened to her, as I was distracted by thoughts about what was going to happen to me.

We walked into Block 11, the punishment block, went down the central corridor, then turned right and down a flight of stairs into the basement. We went along another corridor, through an iron gate and then to the very back of the building. There, we confronted four wooden doors, less than half the height of a normal door.

'These are *Stehbunker* (standing cells),' said Grese. 'Mandel has ordered that you will spend seven nights in these cells. During the day you will work.'

She instructed me to squat down and make my way into one of the standing cells, then closed the door behind me. For a short time I was alone in this very small room. Standing in the centre I could reach out and easily touch all four walls. It was pitch black except for a tiny glow of light coming from a small grate – an air vent – near the roof. When I was later joined by three other prisoners, I understood why this was called a standing cell. With four of us in this tiny space, there was just enough room for us to stand. Even in the wagons during our transport we had room to sit on the floor for short periods, but here there was no space for that. We could barely move our arms, and certainly not lift them. We all ached and moaned our way through the night. It was truly horrific. Only the devil could invent a punishment like this.

Next morning the door opened and we were released from this torture. The other three girls, like most who were sentenced to these cells, were sent off to outside *Kommandos*. Grese told me my job would be to clean the latrines in the surrounding blocks.

After the others had been led away, Grese, speaking quietly, said, 'Lie down quickly before the roll call. Otherwise you won't get through the day.'

'Thank you, Irma,' I said.

'Never mind.'

I have no memory of the roll call that morning, or any other morning that week. I struggled through the job I had been given, dazed and overwhelmed, until I came across a group of male prisoners doing some other work in the building. The words 'standing bunker' were enough for them to take pity on me.

'Lie down and rest,' one of them said. 'We will keep a look out for the SS, and we will clean the latrines for you.'

Another one gave me some food he had saved.

I tried not to think about the night ahead.

But the night came, and I was back in the standing cell. And the nights and days repeated until my sentence was up. I clung to my sanity. Different girls came and went from the cell with me. I know I only survived because I was doing inside work and had the help of these men, who found me each day to let me rest. Many of the girls sent to outside work during the day did not return; they probably died of exhaustion, or were executed for not doing their work.

On the last day I was lying down near the latrines while the men cleaned around me.

'SS coming!' yelled one of them.

I stood up quickly as the men dispersed. Not having time to pretend I was working, I sat on the nearest toilet as if using it.

The SS officer asked me what I was doing.

'Ich scheiße,' I said. 'I'm shitting.'

'I've been looking for you,' he said.

He told me his name was Tauber and that his friend was the *Blockführer* at Birkenau – the one to whom I had given the doll.

'I need a *Blockälteste*,' he said.

7

Back to Birkenau

September 1943

The whistles sounded at 4.30 in the morning, every morning. With that, everyone in the camp was to get off their beds at once. There would be a rush to the latrines or washhouses – thousands of women at once, clambering over and around each other in their hurry to make use of the short time available before the second whistle. If they were lucky, there would be time to use one of the crude toilets (no more than holes over an open pit) and return for some lukewarm tea back at their barrack.

When the second whistle blew, there was another rush, this time to get outside and line up in rows of five in front of the barrack for *Zählappell*. Those too slow to get outside could be beaten by a guard or attacked by one of their dogs. Sadly, some of the *Blockältesten* – particularly the non-Jewish criminal prisoners – joined in this cruelty.

Outside, regardless of the weather, we all stood and waited for the count. We stood in mud or snow. We stood in rain, hail or blistering heat. And standing was a good day. Standing allowed the girls to link arms, to hold each other up, sometimes to sway gently to ease the burden of having to remain in one spot. On other days, an SS guard would order an entire group to kneel rather than stand, sometimes also instructing them to hold their arms straight above their heads. The SS called this *Sport machen*, 'making sport'. In the cruellest cases, women would be made to hold rocks above their heads, badly injuring themselves if the rocks were allowed to fall.

All this could go on for hours. First we waited until the guards were ready to count. Then we waited until they got the count right. If the numbers on the roll didn't match the number of heads counted, they would want to know why. They would re-count. They would inspect the barracks for sick women and those who had died in the night. There were always some. They would slow the count deliberately, just to make us suffer. Not until all the counts of all the blocks in the camp had been completed would we be released.

Standing or kneeling like this for hours, twice a day, every day, would be almost impossible for a fit, well-nourished person. But for people who had been starved and worked to the edge of death, it was often too much. Women would collapse, dead, as we waited. If someone dropped dead during the count, it would have to start again. Anyone who showed signs of weakness or illness – anyone deemed not capable of work – would be selected out to be disposed of via the gas chambers and crematorium.

When the count was finally done, everyone dispersed to their work, whether with an outside *Kommando* or to one of the various inside jobs. For some, their work started with the immediate task of gathering up the bodies of those who had died during *Zählappell*.

All this happened morning after morning, and evening after evening. We could see through the wire that this was all happening in the men's camp as well.

It's difficult to convey the brutality of just a single roll call, let alone the torture of the ceaseless repetition, day after day after day. For months, and then years. *Zählappell* was designed to dehumanise us, to make us suffer and to reveal those too sick or too weak to work. To thin the numbers. Another small step towards the annihilation of the Jews.

For those of us lucky enough to survive, *Zählappell* was a constant in our lives from our arrival in 1942 until the end of the war. The only significant break I had from it was for the period I was in Block 10, where the count was mostly performed inside the building. As a *Blockälteste* in Birkenau, my role was to ensure the lines stayed straight during the long wait for the count to start. At least I was able to move around a little during this time. Once the count started, I would stand at attention next to the SS officer overseeing the process, until it was finally complete.

———

The job Tauber needed me for was as *Blockälteste* of the *Stabsgebäude*, the so-called 'elite' block. This was a wooden barrack outside the main women's camp – officially a separate sub-camp – that accommodated the 360 women who were the secretarial staff of the SS officers. They were prisoners, but they were not subject to the same murderous brutality as the rest of the prisoner population. Almost all were non-Jews – there was just one Czech Jewish girl, named Leah, who was a *Läuferin*, a runner.

When I first entered the block, the women took no notice of me. I observed how relaxed they were compared with the girls in the women's camp. The elite girls' living conditions were hardly comfortable: their barrack was still cold and their bedding provided little padding or warmth. But discomfort is easier to cope with when you aren't living with the constant threat of instant death. They wouldn't be shot for looking at a guard the wrong way. They were never sent to the gas chamber and up the chimney for the crime of becoming ill, nor for any other reason.

For *Zählappell* they would dawdle outside, taking as much time as they felt like to form rows. Their 'rows' were loose as they chatted and joked with one another. They were never expected to kneel or hold their hands in the air. When the guards arrived to count them, they too adopted this relaxed attitude and, as a result, there were frequent errors in the count.

After a couple of days these girls were still ignoring me. I took a whistle that Tauber had given me, moved to the centre of the barrack and blew the whistle loudly. The room fell silent.

'I have been given the job to be your *Blockälteste*. I didn't ask for this position. SS Tauber ordered me to take it. So here I am. I'm going to help you as much as I can. If you want something from me, I can help you. I want us to make this place as nice and clean as possible. But you have to behave properly. I have seen you joke around when it's roll call. When you do that it delays the count for everyone. You don't seem to care that other tired, hungry prisoners have to stand waiting for much longer because of you.'

The girls were quiet.

'From now on,' I said, 'I want you to get outside quickly when the call to *Zählappell* is made. I want you to line up in straight rows of five and help make sure the count is completed as quickly as possible. We are not going to prolong the roll call for others who have it much harder than you.'

The next morning the girls did as I asked and the *Zählappell* was completed more quickly.

As I had when I was appointed to Block 10, I managed to bring together a group of the younger Slovak girls to help me in the elite block, acting as *Stubenältesten*, *Stubendienster* and *Läuferinnen*. This helped me because we could speak our own language, and it helped them because it allowed them to escape outside work.

Now I needed them to help me with a different task. After the girls in the barrack had gone to their work in the camp offices, my helpers and I gathered up all the old blankets from the barrack. We found some trolleys and used these to push our load of blankets over to the storeroom, where I reported that Tauber had ordered me to replace these 360 blankets with new ones. Tauber had not issued this order, but I knew very well by then that the storeroom staff wouldn't check with him. It was enough that I was *Blockälteste* of the elite block, and that I knew Tauber's name. We wheeled the new blankets back to the barrack and laid them out on all the sleeping platforms.

When the girls returned that night and saw their new bedding, they couldn't believe it. There was a lot of animated chatter.

But when the whistle went for roll call that evening, and from then on for the rest of my time with them, they fell quickly into line and obeyed orders.

This was my life as a *Blockälteste*: trying to find small ways to improve conditions, whether that meant new blankets or saving a few minutes from the roll calls.

———

After a while in this elite block I was moved back to the main women's camp in Birkenau. Over the next few months I would move around a few different blocks, wherever Katja asked me to go, as she did what she could to follow the orders given to her by *Schutzlagerführerin* Maria Mandel while also surreptitiously minimising the pain of the prisoners. Sometimes I would be *Blockälteste* and sometimes second in charge.

After the elite block I spent a short time with a block of *Mischlinge*, half-castes, as they were known then. These were mostly children who the SS had decided were half Jewish. They were of various nationalities, including Italian, Greek and French. There were also some pregnant women in this block.

I did not know why these children and new mothers were being kept. It seemed strange, as they were unable to work, and normally the SS were not interested in anyone who was unable to contribute labour. That was why the old and infirm and most children were sent straight to the gas chambers on arrival. There were rumours that a doctor called Josef Mengele was doing some experiments on children, but I had heard no detail, and I hadn't yet crossed paths with Mengele.

Soon afterwards, I was called in front of an SS commander – I think his name was Böhm – and told that an entire Russian village was about to arrive.

'They are not Jews, but they will be our prisoners,' said the commander. 'If the Russians agree to release a high-ranking officer they have captured, the village will be allowed to return.

'I see from your papers that you are a kindergarten teacher. I want you to take charge of the mothers and their children and the older women. Younger single women will be kept in a separate block.'

I thought about how dreadful this place was for everyone, let alone young children. And with the weather now growing colder it would be even worse.

'*Herr Kommander*, this is no place for children. I request that these children be allowed to wash every day to avoid disease, that the roll calls are held inside and that they are provided with good food.'

'It will be so,' he said.

The Russians arrived and I was assigned to Block 2, which housed the mothers, children and the elderly. As they learnt that their conditions would not be as bad as the rest of the camps, the Russian women became very grateful, promising that they would take me to meet *Batushka Stalin*, papa Stalin.

Others weren't so pleased with me, however. All of a sudden, I was to have another brush with death.

The single Russian women were housed next to us in Block 3. Their *Blockälteste*, who was a non-Jewish German, was very jealous of the conditions I had created for my barrack – which she was reminded of every morning and evening when we stayed inside during *Zählappell*. She made up some lie about me to Mandel and I was pulled out of the barrack so she could take over. I was marched, through the first snow of the season, to another block and pushed inside to join a group of other Jewish prisoners. I had nothing, not even a blanket. A few hours later Stasa, a Polish friend, found out where I was and brought me a pillow and a blanket. She told me she would try to get me out of this block. That seemed unlikely the following morning after roll call, when those of us without assigned work were told we were to be taken to the *Revier* to be sterilised by radiation. For me this immediately brought back memories of Block 10 and those girls who never returned after being subjected to Dr Schumann's experiments. Once again I had to face the idea that perhaps this was my end. We were marched to the *Revier*, where one of the doctors' assistants recognised me. When the doctors came into the room to start their work, this assistant told them that the pipes were frozen, so they would not be able to perform any sterilisations that day. With this simple lie, this man saved my life and, temporarily at least, the lives of the women I was with.

In the meantime, Stasa kept watch over what was happening in Block 2. When she saw a man go into the barrack, she ran and found Margot Drechsler, Mandel's assistant. Stasa couldn't speak German, but she gestured furiously to Drechsler while saying in Polish, *'chodź chodź'*, 'come come'. Drechsler followed her to Block 2, where Stasa pointed her inside. There, Drechsler surprised the new *Blockälteste* and her lover, the man Stasa had seen entering the block.

'Get out, disappear,' Stasa heard Drechsler shout at the man.

To the *Blockälteste* she said, 'You pushed Magda out by lying and now you will pay. You're going to the *Strafkommando*.' The punishment brigade.

Then to Stasa she said, 'Bring Magda back.'

Stasa didn't understand the words, but she understood my name and what Drechsler was asking. She was almost out of breath when she found me and, with pride in her voice, said, 'Magda, you're to go back to Block 2.'

The Russian women and children were overjoyed to see me back with them. Some of them even lifted me onto their shoulders as everyone shouted, 'Magda is back, Magda is back!'

Some time later a runner arrived with a message announcing that all Russian boys fourteen years old and younger would be going on a truck the next day. This created enormous anxiety amongst the mothers, of course. No one knew what was going to happen to the boys.

On the camp road I approached Irma Grese and asked her if she knew anything.

'Magda, don't you bother with that. They're going to be adopted by Germans – mostly farmers who don't have any children. They'll be treated well, help the farmers and after a few years of Germanisation they won't even remember they were once Russians.'

Sadly, there was nothing I could do to stop the boys being taken away. However, I was able to organise some pieces of cloth, some string and pens. We wrote the full name of each child on one of these pieces of cloth and tied it with string around his neck, hiding the cloth under his shirt. To each boy I said something like, 'Misha, you must remember you have an older brother Ivan. You are fourteen. You can remember your brother and the rest of your family. When the war is finished, you must announce that you are Russian and that you want to go back to your parents.'

What happened to these boys and whether any of them did eventually find their homes, I never knew.

Eventually, I was moved on to look after another barrack. Over time most of the younger Russian women were also taken away, apparently to work as nurses in German-run hospitals. I never found out what happened to the older women and their men, who had been held in the men's camp.

———

Occasionally in a quieter moment I found myself reflecting on the times I had found the *chutzpah* and courage to speak up to the SS, such as I had done with Dr Wirths, and more recently with Commander Böhm about the conditions for Russian children. I knew I never thought about these things in advance – something drove me forward at the time it was needed. Was this also part of the Belzer rabbi's mission for me?

There was another such instance in late 1943, as the weather started to grow colder. It started with a strange story brought back to me by a Slovakian girl who worked with a very large, friendly German woman known as Poof Mama. Poof Mama – no one knew her real name – had been the madame of a bordello before the war. Now she was in charge of a newly completed sauna at Birkenau, officially the *Entwesungsanlage*, or disinfection facility, the building where incoming prisoners were processed.

Not long after we were moved from Auschwitz I to Birkenau in autumn 1942, we had been issued with cloth dresses to replace the old Russian uniforms we had received on our initial arrival. These were plain, grey dresses, and each girl received just one. In this dress we were to live and work and sleep. We were given no underwear; this dress was all we had to keep warm.

Perhaps because so few prisoners survived Auschwitz–Birkenau more than a few months, no one ever thought to replace these dresses, so around fifteen months later, for those of us who had survived, our dresses had been worn threadbare by rain, sun and dirt. They would provide no warmth at all over the coming winter.

Some of the girls started to tear up old blankets to patch their dresses or to wrap around themselves as crude undergarments. While doing her work in the sauna, the Slovakian girl had become upset by a rumour that all the Slovakians were to be sent to the crematorium because of the damage they were doing to the blankets.

The girl told me that when she had explained her distress to Poof Mama, Poof Mama had said, 'Don't be upset, *Liebchen*,' then headed off, saying, 'I'll be back soon.'

After a while she returned and said to the girl, 'Don't worry. It's taken care of. I went to *Lagerführerin* Mandel and told her, "If you dare do anything to my Slovakian girls, I'll tell all the male commanders you were the best whore in my bordello." Mandel begged me not to say a word. I think we can depend on her silence.'

We never did discover whether there was any truth behind this, but the threat against us went quiet for a while. However, one way or another word of the damaged blankets ended up getting out anyway. A sudden order came for all the Slovakian girls to go to the sauna. There were only around 300 of us left alive by then – 300 of over 7000 who had been transported in 1942 – and virtually all of us were in some sort of functionary role: cleaning, cooking, *Stubenälteste*, *Blockälteste* and so on. Having some sort of function played a big role in survival, mainly because it allowed you to work with other girls in other roles and help each other out. On this occasion, however, we wondered if our unity might work against us. Why were we going to the sauna?

The 300 of us walked into the large hall of the sauna building. Now there was a long table, and seated behind it were a number of high-ranking SS officers. In the centre I recognised *SS-Obersturmführer* Franz Hössler, who had been at Auschwitz for a number of years and had a reputation for extreme heartlessness. While I had been in Block 10, Hössler had created a brothel in the Auschwitz main camp, recruiting non-Jewish women prisoners, or those who he regarded as Aryan, to work in this place in return for better conditions. By now he had worked his way up to the position of *Schutzhaftlagerführer* in charge of the women's camp, working alongside Maria Mandel in this role. Beside him was *Schutzhaftlagerführer* of the men's camp, *SS-Obersturmführer* Johann Schwarzhuber.

Hössler accused us all of damaging German property by tearing up blankets.

'That is sabotage,' he said. 'For that, you will all be sent to the gas chambers.'

With that, 300 hearts sank.

I stepped forward. The girls behind me tried to pull me back, but I ignored them.

'*Dreiundzwanzig achtzehn* (2318) is reporting,' I said, clicking my heels.

Perhaps stunned by my insolence, Hössler said nothing. I took his silence as permission to speak.

'With respect, Commander, these prisoners received the dresses we are wearing over one year ago. We have worked in them, slept in them, stood in them for roll call in sunshine and rain. These dresses are now worn out and, as it is getting colder, it is human nature that some of the girls have tried to protect themselves a little, even if that means tearing off a piece of old blanket. If you were in such a situation, you would do the same. If we were able to be issued with replacement dresses, there would be no need to harm German property any longer.'

I stepped back into line.

Hössler glared in silence for a moment, his face reddening.

'You insolent Jew!' he screamed. 'You will be the first to go up the chimney. You—'

'She is not only an insolent Jew,' interrupted Schwarzhuber, 'but she has something in her head. These women will get new dresses.'

Now Hössler turned his stare to Schwarzhuber, but he dared not criticise him in front of us. He said nothing as Schwarzhuber told us to return to camp.

After the new dresses were issued the next day, I was hugged over and over until I ached.

How did I find the courage to speak up again? Perhaps after nearly two years at Auschwitz–Birkenau I was able to understand the SS mind a little better. I did know how valuable we 300 girls were to them. Without us performing our functionary roles, the officers would have been left with a big headache. Or perhaps, once again, something else was driving me forward.

———

At the end of 1943 I was exhausted. I had been constantly on edge for months. First I had been *Blockälteste* of Block 10, then, after the torture of the standing cell, I had been *Blockälteste* again in a number of different barracks with women of various nationalities, including the Russians and all their children and babies. With every new transport I needed to make sure the new arrivals learnt the ways of the camp so they would have the best chance of survival. I did this while they adjusted to the shock of the terrible world they suddenly found themselves in . . . and while also making sure to obey the orders of the SS to the letter and to never appear too soft.

I asked Katja if I could rest a little, and she found me a job in the camp office with Zippy. The camp office was in Block 4, with the office at one end and accommodation for those of us who worked there at the other.

I knew Zippy quite well. She had also arrived on the second transport, and had assisted Katja with the task of record keeping for much of the time since. Katja and Zippy devised a system with which they saved many lives. When there was a selection, their job was to copy the tattoo numbers of prisoners selected for the gas onto a master list. As they did this, they would replace the numbers of living prisoners with those who had already died. The SS never counted the number of people actually on a truck: they just wanted the master list. If it had enough numbers on it, they were happy.

Zippy was a graphic designer so was valuable for those skills. Early on she had the job of painting red stripes onto civilian clothes that were to be repurposed as camp uniforms. (This was after the SS had used up all the old Russian military uniforms and before the well-known 'striped pyjamas' were used.) Now she was in charge of the *Hauptbücher*, registers or ledgers, which were large books in which prisoner details were recorded. She had to record, in her neatest handwriting, a cause of death for each tattooed prisoner sent to the gas chambers, including their tattoo number. She was not permitted to write the real reason for the person's passing away, which was murder by gassing in most cases. Instead, she had to invent an illness: heart attack, typhus, pneumonia, diphtheria and so on.

(Irma Grese had once taken great pride in telling me, 'We are sure we will win the war. Nobody will believe any stories about the gas chambers because we have a complete register for the women's deaths. You see, Magda, we are clever!' She would eventually be proved wrong, for ultimately, instead of keeping this fraudulent 'evidence', the SS would destroy it all.)

The worst part of this job was that these registers were sometimes filled out in advance of a selection, meaning Zippy was making up causes of death for people who had not yet died. Many, of course, were not known to her. Many had arrived at Birkenau very recently. But she did know some of those on her lists, and she might still see these doomed people in the camp – 'a living body in front of me, who I know will be dead tomorrow or the day after' she told me once. Yet, like all of us, she was completely powerless to do anything to alter their inevitable fates in the face of the SS's murderous system.

I worked alongside Zippy doing this work, recording registration entries in my neatest handwriting, over the winter of 1943/1944. Then, in spring 1944, my relative peace was broken when Katja came to me saying that a number of transports would soon be arriving with thousands of Hungarians, and that Mandel wanted me to work in a functionary role again. None of us knew, of course, that we were about to experience the most murderous period of Auschwitz–Birkenau's dark history.

8

Lagerälteste

Katja took me and six other women, mostly Slovaks, to Birkenau sector B-IIe, which was known as the 'gypsy camp'. The Nazis saw the Romani people, or gypsies as they were known then, as 'unclean' in a similar way to the way they saw the Jews, and many thousands of them were rounded up and sent to Auschwitz for slave labour and extermination. The Romani had been isolated in this sector, not mixing with any other prisoners. Now, however, seven of the thirty or so barracks within B-IIe had been emptied out – presumably through mass execution – in readiness for the arrival of Hungarian transports.

Katja spoke to us. 'You have been selected to be *Blockältesten* for the Hungarians because you speak Hungarian and German.'

She went on to allocate blocks to us. I would have Block 1. Anna Brechta was given Block 4. Vera Fischer would have Block 7. And so on.

Vera and I were friends by then, but had come to know each other in an unusual way. She was a fellow Slovakian who had arrived at Auschwitz about two weeks after me. One time quite early on, in Block 9 at Auschwitz main camp, I discovered that she had scratched some words into the wood of her bunk bed. I gave her a slap, telling her that she was destroying German property and that if this was discovered she and possibly others would be punished. Vera was shocked by my response, but she understood why I did it. She explained that she had been trying to record the words of a song that had come into her mind. Once I knew this I organised some paper and a pencil so that she could write out the song properly. I don't remember it anymore and the paper disappeared long ago, probably not long afterwards. But it was the start of our friendship. I advised Vera that she should wait for her soup at the back of the line, and would then get more of the vegetables from the bottom of the kettle. Like me, Vera had eventually become a *Blockälteste* in Birkenau.

Once Katja had organised us in our blocks, she announced that I would be the one in charge of this group of seven barracks. She also told us there was a new *Kommandant* of the Birkenau complex, *SS-Hauptsturmführer* Josef Kramer, who had a reputation for murderous cruelty. It would be best if we maintained order and avoided SS attention.

Soon after, the Hungarians started to arrive.

———

While we had done what we could to survive Birkenau since August 1942 as the SS abused, tortured and murdered their way through the original women's and men's camps, sectors B-Ia and B-Ib, it was obvious they had much bigger plans.

From inside our camp we had watched as four chimneys rose above the new gas chambers and crematoriums. Thirty huts were built as a new *Effektenlager*, the warehouse known by the prisoners as Kanada, to store goods confiscated from prisoners after their arrival. This Kanada was much larger than the first one at Auschwitz I main camp. It was ready for use in late 1943, about the time a new sauna was also opened. Just outside our camp, a railway siding and ramp, or unloading area, was built. When that was complete in May 1944, it allowed transports to enter right inside the complex, where previously they had stopped on the main line a few hundred metres away, at what was called the 'Judenrampe'. Now trains could be more quickly emptied of new arrivals and the initial selection conducted. Better still for the SS, those selected for immediate execution no longer needed to be transported to the gas chambers by truck. Having been told they would be receiving a shower, they could simply walk to their fates.

All of these facilities would allow the processing of many more prisoners. The Nazis' dream of a 'death factory' was coming to fruition.

Across the main road we saw hundreds of new barracks being built behind electric fences, stretching into the distance. Sector B-IIe, the gypsy camp where Vera, myself and the others were now, was part of this expansion.

When the Hungarian transports started arriving in May, they came in the thousands. Until this time there had been very few Hungarians at Auschwitz–Birkenau, as Hungary did not support the Germans in deporting its Jews as Czechoslovakia and other countries had. But after Germany invaded Hungary in the spring of 1944, all that changed. Nearly half a million Jews would be transported out of Hungary over the next two months, most of them to Auschwitz.

After trains arrived at the new siding, we would see hundreds of people lined up on the ramp. We could see the selection take place, with most people, especially women with children and the elderly, sent left . . . straight to the gas chambers and crematoriums.

The younger women capable of work were processed in the sauna then came to us at the gypsy camp, a few hundred at a time. Just as we had been when we first arrived over two years earlier, they were lost, confused and frightened, with no idea what was happening to them or their families.

One Sunday soon after the first Hungarians had arrived in the gypsy camp, my cousin Aliska, a *Läuferin*, came looking for me.

'Magda, come quickly. The girls in Block 1 want to go with Dr Klein. He told them they will go to a sanatorium.'

I followed Aliska back to the block and there was Dr Fritz Klein, a tall, thin, bespectacled man who was a camp doctor, speaking to a large group of girls in perfect Hungarian, telling them how beautiful they were and that they didn't need to put up with these camp conditions.

'Why should you be in this camp?' he said. 'I'll send you to my sanatorium. Everything is there. It's nice and clean. There are gardens and good food.'

The girls were pushing each other as they tried to get to the front so that Klein would pick them to go with him. Amongst them I noticed another cousin, whose name was also Magda – Magda Englander. Magda had a permanent limp that, if noticed by the SS, would have been a death sentence. This would certainly have happened if she had been sent to an outside *Kommando*, so to avoid this I had been trying to find her some inside work.

Of course I had seen Klein's game before. Vera and I had seen it many times. This was one of the cruel tricks the SS liked to play with new prisoners. Klein had no sanatorium. He was trying to deceive the girls with the promise of better conditions, but his real intention was to send them to their deaths in the gas chambers. It didn't matter that these girls were young, healthy and able to work. In his eyes, there would be plenty more arriving soon.

Ever since they had arrived we had tried to tell the girls not to believe the promises of the SS. We had often pointed to the chimneys and said, 'That is the only way they will allow you to leave this camp.' But Klein's sweet talking to the girls in their own language was enough to convince them otherwise. They wanted to go.

I pushed my way to the front of the group, raised my hands and shouted, 'You are not going to a sanatorium and leaving me here to rot away in this camp. If I have to stay here, so do you.'

I pointed at the barrack.

'Go back, go back. Back inside.'

Some of the girls turned around, but others complained. 'Why do you have to be so mean?' they said, glaring at me.

Some became hysterical. Some – including my cousin Magda – were so desperate to go with Klein that I had to slap them across the face to bring them to their senses. If a slap was needed to save their lives, it was a small price to pay.

I turned around to Klein.

'You have no business being here today. *Kommandant* Kramer will be very angry with you if he finds out. So leave now and don't try this again.'

Klein reached for the gun on his belt, but then changed his mind. He turned and walked away. My *chutzpah* had worked again, though inside I shook with relief.

Some of those girls, including Magda, held a grudge against me after that. They never thanked me for saving their lives; all they remembered was that I had slapped them.

————

Transports carrying Hungarian Jews continued to arrive one after the other. Soon our seven blocks were completely full, even allowing for the obscene overcrowding that the SS expected. Smoke rose from all four crematorium chimneys all day, every day.

Katja came to me and said, 'Everyone will be moving to sector B-IIc – they call it *C Lager*, Camp C. Mandel is going to tell you that you will be *Lagerälteste*, in charge of the whole camp.'

'Katja, have mercy on me. I can't do that. Please select somebody else.'

I tried to find an excuse that would release me from such a burden.

'Even if I come out of this alive, how could I possibly keep thousands of women happy? How many enemies would I make?'

'It's not my decision,' she said. 'And anyway, the underground want you to do it. They know you will try to help whoever you can. Would you rather Stenja did it? You know she is brutal.

She will do nothing but send women to the gas chamber as soon as she can.'

I wasn't happy. I did not want to take on so much responsibility.

A little while later Margot Drechsler, who was still an assistant to *Lagerführerin* Mandel, called me over.

'Hellinger. You will be the *Lagerälteste* in Camp C,' she said.

'Please don't make me *Lagerälteste*,' I said. 'I don't know how to be one.'

'Of course you don't, Magda. There has never been a Camp C.' She laughed.

The next day the call went up, 'Magda to the front.'

I walked to the gate at the front of our camp where I found a large black car waiting, its back door open. Inside was *Kommandant* Kramer.

I clicked my heels. '*Dreiundzwanzig achtzehn* (2318) is reporting,' I announced.

'Hellinger,' he said. 'Get in.'

I knew Kramer from his reputation, which had circulated the camp since he arrived. A very large man, during his time as commandant of another concentration camp he had apparently killed at least one person by squeezing their neck with his enormous hands before dropping them to the ground and stepping over them.

We sat in silence as the car drove around 500 metres up the road to another camp. We got out and looked at the two long rows of barracks stretched out in front of us. He gazed down at me.

'Here you will be *Lagerälteste*,' he said.

I estimated there were thirty blocks. (There were actually thirty-two.) If each contained 1000 prisoners, I would be responsible for over 30,000 people. A city inside an electric fence.

We walked to the first accommodation block and I looked inside. There were sleeping stalls, but otherwise it was completely empty.

'*Herr Kommandant*, here you want me to be *Lagerälteste*?' I said. 'But the barrack is empty. There is no straw for bedding, no blankets, no bowls or spoons. If these women are to live like this, your guards will call them Jewish swine. It would be better to send them to the gas chambers straight away.'

'Why do you care so much about others? Care about yourself,' he said.

'If the situation was reversed and you were in charge of the German prisoners and didn't try to help them, some would call you a coward.'

He glared at me for a moment, then looked me up and down. I didn't move. I just stood straight and held his gaze. Somehow I was sure he was trying to find a sign of weakness, but I wouldn't show him any.

'Supplies will come tomorrow,' he said.

Inside Camp C were already 8000 male prisoners. A few SS officers were discussing how to move the men to the adjacent men's camp, sector B-IId known as Camp D, without causing confusion and disorder by having the men cross paths with the women coming in the opposite direction from the gypsy camp.

'I can organise it, if you will allow me to take charge,' I said. They agreed.

I walked to Camp D and found the *Lagerälteste*.

'I need to bring 8000 men here. To maintain order, we will bring 1000 at a time.'

Magda's house at 18 Masarikova Ulica Michalovce, Czechoslovakia.

A Burger family wedding, approximately 1928. Magda is standing second from the right in a light coloured dress. Her mother Berta is fourth from the right. Sitting on the mat, first from the right: cousin Irena, who Magda had to slap to get her off the cart during the death march from Auschwitz. Also sitting, second from left: Piri, Irena's sister.

Magda with her brother Max in their back garden, sometime in the 1930s.

Magda's brother Max Hellinger.

Magda's brother Eugene Hellinger.

Magda's brother Ernest Hellinger.

Magda (R) at the 1935
Fourth World Convention
of Hashomer Hatzair
(Jewish Scouts), in Poprad.

Magda with unknown friend in
Slovak army uniform, 1941.

Magda's cousin Aliska who was only 14 years old when sent to Auschwitz. She acted as a runner for Magda.

1939. Béla's son Ervin (L), who perished with his mother Irma in 1942, and Bela's nephew Tommy (R). Ten-year-old Tommy was a constant companion of Magda as they waited for Béla to come back to his home town of Žilina after liberation.

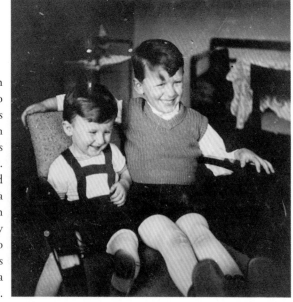

Irma Grese, SS Guard: 'The Beautiful Beast', 'The Hyena of Auschwitz'. (Image © Imperial War Museum.)

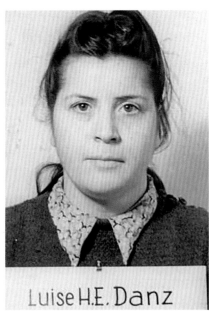

Maria Mandel, SS Guard.

Luise H.E. Danz, SS Guard.

Josef Kramer, SS Commandant of Auschwitz–Birkenau. (Image © Imperial War Museum.)

Dr Maximilian Samuel, Jewish prisoner doctor in Block 10. (Image courtesy of Yad Vashem Photo Archive, Jerusalem.)

Dr Carl Clauberg, SS doctor in Block 10. (Image © Imperial War Museum.)

Dr Eduard Wirths, chief physician at Auschwitz from 1942.

A letter from Magda to Philip Reich, the brewery owner in Michalovce, sent from Birkenau, April 1943. Unsure of the fate of her family, Magda assumed the brewery would be allowed to continue, no matter what. With this coded letter Magda sent a message to reassure the families in Michalovce that the girls she had listed were still alive.

Postcard from Birkenau to Marta Bandi and Eva, July 1943.

Magda writes: I cannot describe my happiness when I received your dear letter. I am pleased to learn that you are all together at home. Please reassure the boys [Ernest and Eugene] that I am ok. I often think about you and Eva. Do you think about me from time to time? Please write more often, it is so good to hear from you. Please send my regards to all relatives and friends who inquire about me, and many kisses to you. Yours, Magda H.

Postcard sent by Magda from Birkenau to her brother Ernest, who was imprisoned in the Novaky labour camp in Slovakia.

Magda writes: Dearest Ernest, I wrote to you and Eugene through Marta, I would like to hear good news about you. Please write to me, I am well. Please write. Kisses, Magda.

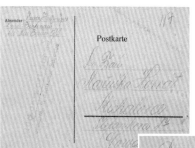

Postcard from Magda to her friend Marta Horvat in Michalovce, Slovakia from Birkenau, 1944.

Magda writes: Dearest, I have received your lovely greetings. I will be extremely grateful if you can help out Ernest and Eugene on my behalf. Greetings to Petku and others. Kisses, Magda.

The certificate to Auschwitz from Kfar Sabah Palestine, August 1944. This is a list of Auschwitz women prisoners for whom the Jewish Agency requested immigration permits to Palestine. The Political Department investigated this with brutal questioning of those on the list. Magda's name at number 2, is highlighted.

Magda's repatriation certificate, 1945 stating her profession as teacher and her intended destination as Michalovce and then Palestine.

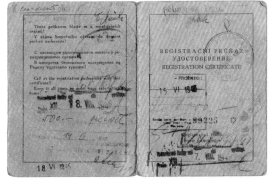

Registration certificate issued in Prague 1945.

Magda in Prague, 1948.

Magda and Béla in Prague, 1948.

Magda in Jiříkov, Czechoslovakia, approximately 1948.

Magda in Jiříkov, Czechoslovakia, approximately 1948.

Magda and Béla, in Jiříkov, approximately 1948.

Béla, Maya and Magda in Jiříkov, approximately 1948.

Magda and Béla, with Magda's brothers Max and Ernest and young Maya shortly after arrival in Israel, 1949. Note the refugee tents in the background. (L to R: Max, Magda, Bela, Maya and Ernest.)

Above: Maya (3 years old) and sister Eva (18 months) in a Ma'abarot refugee camp, Israel, 1949.

Left: Soon after arrival in Israel, 1950. Magda with Maya (L) and Eva.

Magda and helper with kindergarten in Holon, Israel, approximately 1951, celebrating the festival of Purim. Maya standing first on the left, sister Eva standing second from right.

Magda's kindergarten with helper Rachel, Maya standing far right, and Eva second from right.

Magda's kindergarten with helper Rachel in Holon, approximately 1950. Maya standing third row, third from left. Eva sitting third from left.

Magda's childhood friend Marta with husband Bandi Horvath in Argentina, 1952.

Article by Dr Gizella Perl headed 'Magda the Lageralteste camp C' in *Új Kelet*, the Hungarian language newspaper in Tel Aviv Israel, 28 August 1953.

Magda at the memorial plaque for Dr Adélaïde Hautval, at Yad Vashem, Israel's official memorial to the victims of the Holocaust. Adélaïde Hautval was one of the prisoner-doctors with whom Magda had significant dealings at Auschwitz, and they stayed in contact until she died in 1988.

Magda and Béla in 1989, note the numbers on their arms: Magda 2318, Béla 65066.

1988, Magda with Katya Singer the *Rapportschreiberin* in Auschwitz–Birkenau. Magda and Katya would correspond regularly and meet in Prague when Magda travelled.

Magda and Béla, in Hawaii 1993.

In Budapest in 2015 to celebrate Maya and Des's 50th wedding anniversary. From left: granddaughter Arianne Fink Matthaei, Arianne's husband Wanja Matthaei, Maya, Maya's husband Des Lee. From right: granddaughter Alexi Fink, daughter Jenni Lee, son Michael Lee.

And so I started. I arranged for the first thousand men to march in rows of five to their new camp. SS guards kept watch on the road, but they did not need to do anything. I then collected 1000 women from the gypsy camp and they walked to Camp C. Once they were inside a block, the next thousand men moved to their camp. We carried out this process eight times, until all the men and women were where the SS wanted them to be.

The officers were surprised at how smoothly I solved the problem. They seemed a little shocked that a Jewish woman was capable of such organisation. Commandant Kramer looked on with satisfaction.

Now I saw an opportunity.

'Commandant Kramer, if I can work with my *Blockältesten* and other functionaries to keep this camp clean and orderly, will you then keep SS guards out of the camp as much as possible?'

'You will need to work with *SS-Helferin* Grese. She will be the *Lagerführerin* of this camp from tomorrow.'

————

And so we set up Camp C. I worked with Katja to find Slovakian girls, especially those who were doing dangerous work in outside *Kommandos*, and appoint them as *Blockältesten*. Some of those were friends and cousins.

A girl called Elsa Krauss approached me and said she was from my home town, Michalovce. She thought we might be distant relatives. She asked if I could give her some sort of functionary role.

'You are just the girl I have been looking for. I want you to find a hundred or so other girls, as many as you need, and this group will be responsible for the cleanliness of the camp, including the latrines – as clean as we can keep it under the circumstances.'

Block 2 was a kitchen block in one half, while the other half included accommodation rooms for myself – a room of about four metres by two metres – and another room for the Camp C *Rapportschreiberin*, a wonderful girl called Gerda, and for the *Lagerkapo* Surka (who was responsible for organising women for the outside *Kommandos*). The *Blockältesten* of Block 2 and the girls who worked in the kitchen also slept in this half of the building.

A *Stubendienst* was chosen from the Hungarian girls so that she could explain their duties in their own language. As we had ever since we arrived at Auschwitz, each morning groups of girls would carry large kettles of weak tea to the barracks – four girls per kettle. Later they would take bread and, very occasionally, margarine or cheese or salami, and then, in the evenings, the weak, sour-tasting 'soup' with a few vegetables at the bottom.

Initially there were around 7000 women, almost all Hungarians, in this camp – just those who had moved from the gypsy camp. But within days, as more and more transports arrived from Hungary, Camp C quickly filled. Before long my 'city' had grown to its maximum population of over 30,000, all crowded into an area around 800 metres long and 200 metres wide. The conditions were horrific, as so many other survivors have recalled in telling their own stories. Every block was severely overcrowded, 'bedding' was no more than a layer of straw and a thin blanket shared between four or more women. The food was dreadful, as it had been since our own arrival, and there was nowhere near enough to provide adequate nutrition. Every woman was soon reduced to little more than a skeleton.

Death was always close. It should never be forgotten that the period over the summer and autumn of 1944 was the deadliest of the Holocaust. The Nazis murdered close to 400,000 people, mostly Hungarian Jews, in just a few months. Most were gassed immediately after their arrival, but many others died in the weeks and months afterwards. Some just lost hope and fell to the ground, or threw themselves against the electric fence to end it all. For many others, injury during work, disease, malnutrition – any reason for not being able to work – was reason enough for the SS to send a prisoner up the chimney. Not that they needed a reason at all. There were no consequences for an SS guard who chose to simply shoot a prisoner dead for being in the wrong place or for looking at him the wrong way. After all, the aim was genocide, sooner or later. The life of a Jewish prisoner had no value.

How could I make this inescapable hell just a little less hellish?

I was in a position I had no choice but to take, but now that I was in that position I felt the responsibility of 30,000 lives on my shoulders every day. If there was the smallest thing I could do to make things a tiny bit better for the women in this camp, I would do it.

After choosing my *Blockältesten* I gathered them together and told them, 'You have been chosen for this position of *Blockälteste* so that you can do what you can to look after our Jewish sisters. You will have your own room to sleep in and a small amount of freedom, but in return you need to do your utmost best.'

I was insistent that we keep the camp as clean and hygienic as we possibly could in the impossible circumstances. We would work together to prevent or contain disease outbreaks. We would try to maintain order, which would keep us from drawing the attention of the SS guards. We would make sure that *Zählappell* did not last any longer than it needed to. We would ensure that food was distributed fairly and that those who needed it most, whether because they were doing outside work or because they were sick, got a little more if there was enough. We would hide the ill or injured to prevent them from being selected.

If we could do these things, we might save a few lives, or make life a little more bearable. But we had to work together.

'The moment you fail at your duty, you will be punished by me,' I said.

Unfortunately, I did need to use discipline sometimes. Many of these girls were young, and we were asking a lot of them. I started carrying a stick, not to hit people with, but to assert some authority. I also wore a striped jacket that had an armband bearing the letters 'LA', for *Lagerälteste*.

A prisoner came up to me one time and said, 'I have been watching you Magda, how you use your stick. When there is *balagan*, chaos, with girls screaming and screeching and fighting, you take one step forward and hold your stick up and stare at them eye-to-eye and wait until they stop. And somehow they are listening and obeying. I thought I must tell you because if I didn't see it, I wouldn't believe it.'

'I must do it,' I said, 'because if I don't there will be chaos. If there is chaos, the SS will come and start shooting people. Keeping order keeps them away.'

There was no time to be nice about this.

Another time one of the girls screamed, 'The Red Cross is here! The Red Cross is here!'

I don't know what caused her to think this, but it was a false alarm. Nevertheless, pandemonium broke out. Girls were dancing, singing and throwing things, including their soup dishes, around. Terrified the SS would be alerted by the commotion and come into the camp with their guns, I put on my striped jacket and strode into the group with my stick held high.

'Silence!' I called.

Some of the girls retreated a little, while others stopped and looked up at the stick. Some continued their unwarranted celebration.

I shouted again and gradually all became quiet.

'There is no Red Cross,' I said. 'This is some girl's silly joke. It is a dangerous joke. Pick up your soup bowls and return to your barracks. I run this camp with few SS men or women coming here. This saves lives. Remember that, and no one ever do something like this again.'

The crowd dispersed.

The next day when the girls were bringing the soup I heard screaming from one of the barracks. As the kettle was being carried inside, a woman had lifted the lid and dipped her soup bowl in, spilling soup and scorching the hands of the girls carrying the kettle, who were now crying in pain. I hated to do this, but I slapped the woman's face and said, 'You scorched the hands of these girls by spilling some of the soup. And because of what you did, some women won't receive their portions.'

'I did it for my two daughters,' she pleaded.

I felt for her, but replied, 'Others have daughters too.'

One recurring problem was that certain men – prisoners working in a *Kommando* in Camp C – made a habit of appearing in a barrack and using cigarettes to lure girls to the washroom for sex. I couldn't stand that the girls were taken advantage of in this way, and possibly getting pregnant, so I encouraged my helpers to be very strict about stopping it. I approached one of the men and told him that if I found the men who were doing this, I would inform their German *Kapo*. That was a threat most of them heeded, but not all. One day the girls in charge of cleaning the washhouses discovered a girl with a man. They brought her to the office. We wrote on a big sheet of paper, 'I SOLD MYSELF FOR A FEW CIGARETTES!' and told her to kneel while holding the sign. As other girls walked past her, I heard comments like 'Serves her right', 'Shame on her', 'She will give all of us a bad name' and 'This is a camp not a bordello'. I doubt that this stopped the behaviour completely, but it slowed it down.

After a few weeks I noticed that some of the *Blockältesten* were not carrying out their duties properly. Fights were breaking out in their barracks and they were ignoring them, just sitting in their rooms.

I gathered the offending *Blockältesten* together and said, 'Remember I said that you are here for the good of the people? We can't do anything against the SS. We are too weak. But we can do whatever we can to keep order and make sure everyone shares what food is available. Now we no longer have order. I said you would be disciplined so now you will be.'

At the front of the camp was a pond, sort of like a small swimming pool, which was an emergency supply of water in case of a fire.

'I want you to jump like a frog,' I said. 'I want you to jump around this pool a few times. Hopefully it will help you remember my message.'

At first they didn't believe me. We had all been on the early transports and had been at Auschwitz–Birkenau for two years. We were friends.

'Do you really mean this, Magda?' one of them said.

'Did you really mean to ignore the *balagan* in your block? Did you care if it caused the SS to come and cause trouble? You might be angry at me now, but when you think about it you will know that you deserve this. You didn't think about your sisters.'

And so the girls frog-jumped around the pool a few times. It ended up in laughter, but I didn't mind that. They got the message.

Many of the Hungarian women saw me running around the camp, carrying my stick and raising it at times, speaking harshly to some people and, occasionally, slapping someone on the face to bring them into line. These women did not understand that it was possible for things to be so much worse. They had not experienced the complete chaos of our arrival two years before or the muddy filth of the unfinished camp we found at Birkenau six months later. They couldn't see the small improvements we were able to make to their lives. They couldn't appreciate the difference it made just having some of us around who already knew how the camps worked. Instead of believing the many lies of the SS, they could rely on us to help them adapt to the surrounds, as shocking as they were. As most of us in functionary roles were Slovakian, there was also a cultural distrust.

For centuries, Hungarians had looked down upon the Slovaks as uncultured, uneducated peasants. This was made worse after the fall of the Austro-Hungarian Empire, when Hungary lost a large part of its territory to the new nation of Czechoslovakia. None of this had anything to do with us, of course, but it didn't stop many Hungarian inmates from refusing to listen to what we had to say. Instead, many saw those of us in functionary positions and believed we were entitled, that we had more power than we actually did have, or that we were collaborating with the SS. They did not seem to understand that we lived constantly with the sword of Damocles hanging over our heads, that even granting a small kindness could be enough for us to be seen as too soft, and so banished or killed.

Some of these women seemed to see our common enemy – the Nazis – as the lesser evil.

———

As I started to meet more of the women in our camp, I was able to work out whose skills could be put to good use.

A girl came to me and said she was the daughter of the rabbi of the synagogue in Košice, a small city not far from Michalovce. She said she was a gymnast and wanted something useful to do.

'I have been looking for someone like you,' I said. 'I'd like you to find as many of the younger girls as you can each day. Take them to the back of the camp where few will see you, and give them some exercises. It will do their morale and bodies well. If you get hungry, go to the kitchen and tell them I sent you. They will help you.'

One morning, a woman approached me and introduced herself as Dr Gisella Perl. She told me she needed a pair of shoes, so I invited her into my room and gave her shoes and a towel. As it was getting cold, I also gave her a cardigan some girls had organised for me. Gisella told me she was a gynaecologist who had worked in a Romanian sanatorium, so I told her I would put her in the *Revier*.

This soon proved to be a good decision.

An order circulated that all pregnant women were to report for registration before being sent to a sanatorium – which almost certainly meant death. I sent out my runners with the message that pregnant women must not report anywhere and that the *Lagerälteste* would visit them. I then called for Dr Perl and asked her to determine the current number of pregnancies in the camp.

Thankfully there were only a few pregnant women, so I was able to deal with them one by one. I called each of them to see me with Gisella. We explained that being sent to the sanatorium really meant being sent to the gas chambers, but that having an abortion would save their life. Gisella explained to each one that because she was so young, there was only a low risk that having an abortion would prevent her having a child later in life. Of course the women were hesitant. We were forcing them into a dreadful predicament. But we were able to convince most of them. I made them swear that they wouldn't mention this to anybody. If what we were planning was discovered, many more would be sent up the chimney.

We went to the *Revier* and Dr Perl performed the abortions as best she could on the dirt floor, with neither equipment

nor hygiene. Nevertheless, everything went without compli-
cation, each woman resting for a while then returning to her
barracks.

Later we discovered a woman who had managed to hide her
pregnancy. When she was close to giving birth, Gisella helped
her through labour and delivered the child. The mother had a
day's rest in the *Revier* then returned to her barrack. The infant,
who the SS would never allow to stay alive in this place, was
quietly allowed to pass away before any more cruelty could be
imposed on its short life.

Over the coming months Dr Perl would deliver dozens of
babies and perform countless abortions on the floor of the *Revier*.
She saved the lives of many women in this way, though sadly at
the expense of many innocent unborn or newborn children.

Such were the unimaginable dilemmas faced by those of us
who found opportunities to save one life even as thousands of
others were lost.

9

SS connections: Irma Grese

The more I had the chance to observe the prominent SS – people like Eduard Wirths, Josef Kramer and Irma Grese – the more I understood that despite their murderous practices, they were still human beings. I don't say this to excuse their actions in any way, or to suggest that I liked any of these people for even a second. On the contrary, realising that they were human helped me understand that they had human needs and vulnerabilities. This created opportunities. People like myself and Vera Fischer – people who had arrived at Auschwitz on the first transports – learned to talk back to the SS if we were careful and chose our times. There was always fear. Any of them could, at any time, have us killed or kill us themselves. But if we maintained respect, avoided ever telling them what to do and acted with the right amount of *chutzpah*, there were ways we could manipulate them.

There is no better example of this than the way I was able to work with Irma Grese.

After the war, Grese became known as perhaps the most infamous female SS guard. She was young, attractive and earned a reputation for promiscuity and extreme cruelty at the Ravensbrück, Auschwitz–Birkenau and Bergen-Belsen concentration camps. During the so-called Belsen trial in 1945, when charges were heard against Grese, Josef Kramer and forty-three others accused of war crimes at Auschwitz and Bergen-Belsen, Grese became the centre of much of the media's attention. They gave her the nickname 'The Beautiful Beast'. She was only twenty-two years old when she was sentenced to death by hanging. Grese's reputation continued to grow in the following years, and in many accounts she comes across as a one-dimensional monster. Yet the Grese I knew was also a person. Yes, an evil person capable of terrible sadism, but also a damaged young person who, underneath everything, was vulnerable and impressionable.

Irma Grese arrived at Camp C on the day after we moved into the sector. When I saw her walk into the camp, I approached her and reported for duty.

'*Lagerführerin* Grese. I am your *Lagerälteste*. We will try to work together.'

Grese was the only SS guard who was permanently based in Camp C. She had an office in the small guardhouse at the gate of the camp, where there was also a guard on duty at all times who kept watch over who was coming and going.

At least once a day she would seek me out to talk to. We often had conversations like those we'd had back at the *Brotkammer* at the Auschwitz main camp, and it felt like she saw me as a big sister. She would chat to me in the indiscreet way of a young person trying to impress someone older. She sometimes told me about her family: she was one of five children from a regional area of Germany, her father was a farmer and she had lost her mother when she was a young teenager. She told me about her school years in her early teens, during which she had joined the BDM – the *Bund Deutscher Mädel*, or League of German Girls, a female Nazi youth organisation. She was quite proud of this because the organisation was only open to 'genuine' Aryans, and she became very enthusiastic about the 'mission' of the Nazis and the 'dangers' of race 'pollution'. As she told me things like this it was almost as if she had forgotten that she was talking to a prisoner, let alone a Jewish prisoner. She told me that her joining the BDM had caused a split in her family, as her father was very religious and conservative and did not believe in Nazism. He had become even more angry when she eventually joined the SS and, after she returned home to visit one time dressed in her full SS uniform, he had not spoken to her again.

She also told me about her career. She had wanted to become a nurse and had worked in the Hohenlychen Sanatorium with Professor Doctor Karl Gebhardt. I had not heard of the professor, but Grese revered him as a 'saint' of the Nazi party. After the war it was revealed that Gebhardt was one of the earliest doctors to perform experiments on those the Nazis saw as subhuman, such as the Jews and the Roma. However, Grese didn't succeed in becoming a nurse, and eventually left the hospital. She worked in a dairy for a short time before volunteering to join the SS, still only eighteen years of age. She told me that she hadn't known about the concentration camp and that she couldn't have imagined they would be as bad as they were, but that the Nazis had made working in a camp sound appealing. Regardless, once she joined the SS she took to the job with great loyalty. She put a lot of effort into wearing her uniform properly and keeping her appearance smart, unlike most of the other guards. And she did what she had to do to stand out and advance herself. By the time she was assigned to Camp C, at just twenty years old, she had been promoted to the rank of *SS-Oberscharführerin*, the second highest rank available to a female SS officer – something very rare for someone so young.

Occasionally she would also share things she had heard about the Nazis' plans to win the war. She would tell me gossip about the other SS women, none of whom she was friendly with.

I thought sometimes that perhaps this was why she treated me as a big sister and not as a prisoner. I was the only person she could talk to.

While she would appear almost familiar with me, she soon earned a reputation for brutality – and I saw this side of her too. During roll call one day I was standing in front of Block 2. Suddenly two runners came up to me with four very distressed women whose breasts had been split open. It was a terrible sight, the poor women crying out in pain, their breasts bleeding badly. I asked them what happened and who did this to them, but they were too frightened to reply.

One of the runners said, 'This one told me that *Lagerführerin* Grese struck them with her whip.'

I told the *Läuferinnen* to take the women to the *Revier*.

'Tell Dr Perl I sent you and that she should try her best to help these poor women.'

I then found Grese and, making sure no one else could hear me, said, 'What did you do to those poor women? They are in great pain. Their wounds will likely become infected and they will die. Shame on you.'

She lifted her whip.

'I dare you to strike me too,' I said. 'I know you like to see blood. *Ich bin beleidigt.*' 'I'm offended.'

I turned and walked away.

Later, to my astonishment, Grese came to me and said, *'Vergib mir.'* 'Forgive me.'

From then on she rarely showed her sadistic side if I was around, but sadly that side did come out many times. She wanted power and all the luxuries that she could have with it, and that meant outshining all the other female SS in both looks and brutality. There were many other reports of her using her whip or her pistol, or having groups of prisoners 'make sport' during roll call. It was always mysterious to me that she would show me so much respect yet could be so heartless and cruel to so many others, one minute talking to me as a friend and the next minute being a sadistic devil.

———

There were always rumours about Grese's love life. Depending on who you listened to, she had affairs with Mengele and Kramer, amongst many other men, and with a few women as well, including prisoners. These things may have happened. I did hear from Dr Perl one time that she'd been forced by Grese to carry out an abortion on her. But Grese didn't tell me about any of this, and I took no notice. It was nothing to do with me and I had enough to worry about.

However, she did use me as a confidant.

She came to me one day and said, 'Magda, tomorrow I will introduce you to Hatchi, my new boyfriend. You can tell me what you think of him.'

The next day, a *Kommando* from the male camp was doing some work in Camp C. I had got to know one of the men a little, as we had exchanged a few words on previous occasions. This time he knocked on my door and asked if he could speak to me. I beckoned him inside quickly – to be seen together would likely have meant punishment or death for both of us.

'What is it?' I said.

'I admire you very much. If we survive, I would like to get together after the war. Before the war I was a world-famous jazz drummer.'

He promised me a wonderful life touring the world with his music.

At that moment Grese walked in with Hatchi. Grese was surprised to see another prisoner in the room.

'He is working with the *Kommando*,' I said. 'He's a world-famous drummer,' I added, hoping it might distract from the 'crime' of us talking to each other.

'Really? We'll see if he's a drummer,' said Hatchi.

He bent over.

'Here, drum on my bottom.'

The prisoner drummed quickly with his hands, then lifted one of his boots off the ground and used that as a third 'drum', tapping out a complex rhythm.

'Well, he certainly is a drummer.' Hatchi laughed.

The drummer decided this would be a good time to rejoin his *Kommando*. The distraction had worked.

Grese stayed with Hatchi and we talked for a few minutes. As they turned to leave, Grese looked back at me, eyebrows raised in question.

I nodded my approval, then went back to my work. I didn't see the drummer again.

During Grese's trial after the war it would be revealed that she had followed Hatchi, whose real name was *SS-Sturmmann* Fritz Hatzinger, to the Bergen-Belsen camp in early 1945.

Another time Grese came to me and said, 'Magda, come with me to the men's camp.'

'Why do you need me? You can go there anytime you want.'

'There is a man there who I like very much,' she said. 'I want to visit him. If you come it will look like an official visit.'

Again, she didn't order me, but asked me as if I was a friend.

'When will we go?' I asked.

'Tomorrow,' she said.

I realised this was a rare chance for some of the women to exchange messages with their men in Camp D. Usually the only way for male and female prisoners to communicate was if men came into the camp to make deliveries or do work. But this was very limited, and risky. If the opportunity arose, a male prisoner might come over to me and ask me to help his wife or sister or other family member. At times I found a job for a man in our kitchen, which made a big difference to him, even if it was only for a short time. Like the women in the kitchen, they would not have to stand for roll calls or attend selections. They had food and could sneak any leftovers to relatives or friends. In return for my help, they could sometimes help me with some organisation, or passing information on to the men's camp.

As soon as Grese left, I called all my runners together, along with Gerda, the *Rapportschreiberin*. I told them they needed to organise some paper and pencils and to run around all the blocks and tell any woman who had a husband, father or brother in the men's camp that she should write a short message.

'Tell them to write the man's name on it and the block number if they know it and I will try to deliver it,' I said.

The next day I walked with Grese to the men's camp. I carried a wad of messages hidden under my dress.

'You wait here,' said Grese when we were inside the men's sector. I found the *Lagerälteste* and *Rapportschreiber*, who were both Jewish, and told them my plan. With their help we were able to distribute the precious messages, and some of the men who received one were even able to write a reply on the back, which was returned to me.

And so I was able to organise this exchange of messages. It wasn't much, but it was enough for some of the men and women to tell each other that they were alive, which gave them hope and, for a few, a reason to go on.

Grese and I walked back to Camp C making small talk. She looked pleased with herself. She didn't know that I was too.

We repeated this exercise a couple of other times. I have no idea how many times Grese visited the men's camp on her own.

———

With Grese's reputation for acts of brutality, I always had to be careful not to go too far in testing the unusual relationship we shared, and the opportunities it created. The biggest risk I took involved an outbreak of scarlet fever.

The SS developed a simple approach to dealing with disease outbreaks and potential epidemics. Malaria, typhus and scarlet fever were the most common. When even a few prisoners inside a block became ill, they would send the whole block, or even the whole camp, to the gas chambers.

Across the road from our camp was a smaller women's camp known as 'Mexico'. 'Mexico' was a partly constructed expansion of the Birkenau complex, officially known as sector B-III. This camp housed 8000 Hungarian women and girls. Scarlet fever was detected in the group one day and all 8000 prisoners were immediately murdered – whether they had the disease or not.

As soon as I heard about this, I asked my runners to find every woman in Camp C who was a trained doctor and bring them to me. Soon, sixty-six doctors were gathered in front of me.

'There is scarlet fever in the camps,' I told them. 'We have to try to control any outbreak. We will split you up so that there are two doctors in each block. Your job will be to watch the girls and let me know if anyone shows signs of the disease. We will then quarantine those girls in the small room at the back of each block.'

In the unhygienic conditions of the camp, it was only a matter of time before the disease showed up. However, by separating the sick girls quickly, we had a chance to keep it under control.

Now we had to hide the disease from the SS, which meant mainly from Grese. There was no way I was going to allow this entire camp of 30,000 people to be exterminated. The main challenge was dealing with *Zählappell*. We didn't want the sick girls to mix with the healthier girls, which would soon cause an epidemic, but we had to account for the sick girls in the roll call without drawing attention to their absence.

In the end we were saved by the weather. This happened during a heatwave in the summer of 1944.

I went to Grese and said, 'It is so hot. Why don't you rest in Block 2 while I oversee the *Zählappell*?'

'What will Mandel say if she sees me?'

'Don't worry about her,' I said. 'You are the *Lagerführerin* of this camp and you can do what suits you.'

And so it was. With Grese out of sight, I was able to work with my *Rapportschreiberin* Gerda to make sure the rolls balanced properly, whether the women were able to stand outside their barracks or not.

The weather stayed hot for six weeks, and for all of that time I was able to convince Grese to let me do the roll calls on my own. In that time not one girl was sent to the gas chamber because of scarlet fever. My relationship with Grese had helped save as many as 30,000 lives.

There was one other time a little later when something similar happened. This time Grese and I, preparing for another roll call, stood in Block 2 as rain fell heavily outside.

'You don't want to be outside in this rain,' I said to Grese. 'I have a solution. I will send a *Läuferin* to every block with a message to the *Blockälteste*. We will tell them to get all the girls sitting on their bunks in groups of ten, all with their legs hanging over the front. I will run with the *Rapportschreiberin* and we will quickly count the girls in groups of ten. And you will stay dry.'

Grese agreed, and for once the girls in Camp C were spared standing in the rain for *Zählappell*.

———

I discovered that Grese seemed to be more sympathetic when family was involved. Did she miss her own family? It was hard to tell. But, again, this was something I could take advantage of.

Lili Junger was another cousin of mine who had found me not long after she arrived at Birkenau. Like the *Läuferin* Aliska, Lili was still very young, only fourteen or fifteen. When I first saw her in the camp, I had felt very sad that she had not been able to avoid being deported. I wanted to do what I could to protect both Lili and Aliska, which was why I had made Aliska one of my runners. That way I could keep an eye on her. I decided to assign Lili to Grese as her assistant. Lili would run errands for Grese, deliver messages, retrieve supplies and so on. In return, she would have an easier life and access to better food. She would live with us in Block 2, which was safer and cleaner than living in one of the overcrowded blocks.

Grese was walking through Block 2 one day, and casually lifted some of the mattresses as she passed the bunks.

'Whose bed is this?' she demanded.

I looked at what she had found under the mattress. There were all sorts of things under there: cans of soups, salamis, soaps and even perfumes.

'It is my cousin Lili's bed,' I said.

In working for Grese and running her errands, Lili had been able to steal and save all this relative luxury for herself.

'Your cousin needs to be punished,' said Grese. 'If you don't do it, I will slap your face.'

'Don't worry, Irma. She's the one who will be slapped.'

Grese left, and with the help of a runner I moved all except a few items from under the mattress and laid them out on a bench.

When Lili returned sometime later, I confronted her.

'What is all this? How is that you have so much food and soap and things while other women have nothing? I am so ashamed that I gave you this good position where you are safe and can organise all these things but now you are so selfish.

'Grese said she would punish me if I did not punish you, so here is a slap. I hope you have learnt a lesson.'

Like others, Lili would remember nothing of this after the war . . . except the three slaps I gave her. In truth, it was only the fact that she was my cousin that saved her from a much worse punishment. Grese had been known to shoot a woman dead for less.

A few weeks later I was behind Block 2, looking out onto the road that ran between Camp C and the men's camp, Camp D. It was along this gravel road, which was about one kilometre long, that new arrivals – those who had survived selection on the ramp – walked from the railway siding to the sauna for processing, then back to their camp.

A group of newly arrived men was walking along the road still dressed in their own clothes. I thought one looked familiar, though he was dressed in the linen pants, shirt and large linen hat that was typical of hundreds of peasant communities of the time. I stared at him for a moment, then turned away.

'Malkele, Malkele,' I heard someone call. He was calling my Hebrew name.

I looked again and the man said, 'I'm your uncle, Moishe Mendel.'

I noticed then that the man had his son with him, my cousin Shlomo.

'Keep moving, uncle,' I said. 'It is not safe to stop. I will make contact with you. I can help you.'

I had always been fond of Uncle Moishe, but now I was worried about him. He had somehow survived the selection on the ramp, but he was not a young man. If he was sent to work in an outside *Kommando* he wouldn't survive long.

I sent a message to the *Lagerälteste* in the men's camp and organised for Moishe to be placed in a barrack where his duty would be simply to stand outside the door. I don't know why the SS insisted that someone do this, but at least it made it possible for my religious uncle to pray when he wanted. I organised for Shlomo to work in the Kanada warehouse sorting clothing. My connections in the *Brotkammer* ensured that Moishe had some extra bread, as he would not eat the salami or any non-kosher meat. And I organised for another connection who worked with the clothing to give Moishe a larger striped uniform that would help hide his age a little.

After a while I talked to the *Kommando* leader who often brought a group of men to work in our camp. I arranged for him to bring Moishe for one day so that I could see him. I told Grese that my father was coming to work in our camp and asked her permission for him to visit me. She said if he came to my room she wouldn't notice. Moishe came and sat with me in my room and we spoke a little. While he was with me one of the women in the kitchen made some extra soup for him, a proper soup with plenty of vegetables for nourishment. My uncle savoured every mouthful and I took great pleasure watching him.

'My Magda, are you trying to make a young man out of me?' he asked.

'Yes,' I replied. 'You have to look young in this place.'

I was able to help another relative soon after this. I received news around July that my aunt Ester had been brought to Birkenau with her friend Lovy. On arrival they had been put into Block 25 in sector B-Ia, from where they were certain to be taken to the gas chambers. Luckily, Ester asked the *Blockälteste* whether I was in Birkenau, and the *Blockälteste* was able to get a message to me. I told Grese about the situation and was given permission to visit the two ladies, and I then organised with Katja to have them transferred to Camp C, which saved them from the gas chambers, at least for a while. When I visited Aunty Ester again she complained that she had terrible headaches, so I asked Gisella Perl to examine her. Dr Perl discovered that she had a large tumour growing on her brain, which there was no way to treat in this place. Unfortunately, she died after a few months.

Another transport brought a childhood girlfriend, Ruzenka Elefant. When I was a child we had lived for a short time at her grandparents' home and the two of us had become good friends. In the early days of the deportations she had escaped to Hungary with her husband, the Michalovce builder Moskovic. Now she had been caught up in the deportation of Jewish people from Hungary. She was pregnant, but had escaped selection for the gas because she was wearing a big flowing dress that hid her condition.

It must have been easier for Ruzenka to recognise me than the other way around: my hair had grown back a bit, but hers had been hacked off in the sauna. She ran to me and we hugged and kissed.

Later Grese asked me who she was and I said she was my sister. 'How is it she has such dark hair and you are so blonde?' Grese asked.

'She takes after my father and I take after my mother,' I lied.

With Ruzenka, finding a safe job in Birkenau was not going to be enough – her pregnancy put her in too much danger. But I could not countenance the idea of having her end her pregnancy. Instead, I used my connections to have her put on one of the transports to a factory that I had heard was providing better conditions, especially for women.

———

Grese and I were careful not to allow others, especially other SS, to witness our familiarity with one another. Nevertheless, it was obvious to most that Grese showed me respect. Of course, word had also spread of my being invited into Kramer's car, and of my threatening Klein back in the gypsy camp. All of this gave the more junior SS guards the impression that I had some status with the senior SS officers. I didn't. Any of them could have struck me down at any time, especially if I had shown too much familiarity in front of others. Nevertheless, I was able to use this perception to my advantage at times.

One Sunday, Marika, the *Blockälteste* of Block 3, came to speak to me and *Rapportschreiberin* Gerda. She wanted to tell us about a girl called Zsuzsi.

Zsuzsi, just fourteen years old, had arrived with her mother from Hungary. Selected to work, the two had been processed as normal, losing their clothes and hair. They had then been separated and sent to different blocks. Although they were both in Camp C, amongst 30,000 prisoners, all being sent to different jobs, it was very difficult to find one another again. Zsuzsi had asked everyone, but she could not find her mother.

Late one afternoon Zsuzsi was in the washhouse and found herself next to a woman whose head had been badly blistered and swollen, and who also looked sunburnt. Her eyes were hardly visible. The woman looked at her and exclaimed, 'Zsuzsi!'

Zsuzsi had not recognised her own mother.

The two of them embraced with joy. Zsuzsi's mother explained that her head was blistered from the chemicals used for disinfection, and that she had then become sunburnt from outside work.

It was getting dark and Zsuzsi didn't want to risk losing her mother again, so the two of them went to the mother's block, Block 3. Zsuzsi squeezed in beside her mother in the already cramped sleeping space. There was a problem the next morning, however, when during the *Zählappell* there was one extra on the count for Block 3, and of course one prisoner missing from Zsuzsi's block, Block 12. After two re-counts, one of the women who had slept on the same bunk as Zsuzsi and her mother pointed Zsuzsi out as the extra.

As this was on a Sunday, Grese was not in the camp. Instead, it was being overseen by an SS *Blockführerin* called Hasse. She was a very large woman with legs like tree trunks, a face the colour of a radish and unruly hair. She was also violent. She pulled Zsuzsi out of the line and started hitting her with a stick. She kept hitting her while pushing her towards the front gate of the camp. When Zsuzsi collapsed, unconscious, Hasse simply dragged her to the side and left her by the road. Zsuzsi lay amongst the bodies of women who had died in the night and whose corpses would be collected in the morning and taken to the crematorium. Had Zsuzsi not regained consciousness, she would have been taken with them. However, she was roused after it started to rain, and managed to make her way back to Block 3, where she was cared for by her mother and Marika.

After Marika explained all this to me and Gerda, Gerda transferred another prisoner from Block 3 to Block 12, leaving a space for Zsuzsi in her mother's block. She also found Zsuzsi work in the kitchen, where she wouldn't need to stand for roll call and could be kept hidden from Hasse.

By the next Sunday, Zsuzsi had put this experience behind her. Working in the kitchen, she found some leftover potatoes and, checking there were no SS around, she went outside and shared them with a group of women nearby. She saw her mother and beckoned her over, went inside for more potatoes and came out again, sharing these with her mother and some others.

Just as this bowl was about finished, Hasse appeared from nowhere. This time she took her stick to the women who were eating potatoes, including Zsuzsi's mother. A commotion erupted, with women screaming and Hasse growing more and more angry. When I arrived to see what was going on, I saw Zsuzsi wound around Hasse's stick like a snake, trying to prevent her

155

from hitting anyone else. Hasse was so worked up by now that if she had been able to free her stick she would almost certainly have killed Zsuzsi.

'Was geht hier vor sich? Lässt sie los!' I shouted. 'What is going on here? Let her go!'

Hasse stared at me in fury, but she let go of the stick.

She walked away and did not bother Zsuzsi or her mother again.

How could I, a Jewish prisoner, have such influence over an SS guard, even a junior one? Such was the power of my perceived status.

This was not the end of Zsuzsi's pain, however. One very cold morning, a group of women waited near Block 2. They had been selected for transfer to factory work and were waiting for trucks to arrive to transport them. From the kitchen Zsuzsi could see how cold they were getting, so she thought to make some tea for them. As she prepared the hot water, Grese walked past and asked what she was doing.

'I am making tea for the women outside,' said Zsuzsi.

'You want tea?' said Grese. 'Here, you will have tea.'

Grese picked up the pot and threw it at Zsuzsi, spilling boiling water over her.

Zsuzsi screamed. She ran and found me in my room and I took her to the *Revier*, where we managed to find something to relieve her burns.

This was the sort of impetuous, childish, callous act that Grese was capable of. And it showed the limits of any influence I had over Grese. I don't believe she would have done this if I had been in the kitchen, but I couldn't be with her in every room, every time. On her own, unfortunately, Grese was capable of anything.

Despite all this, Zsuzsi survived the war, and she would often talk about the burn scars on her shoulders and hands from this last run-in with Grese.

10

SS connections: Kramer and Mengele

The relative quiet of Sundays, with no outside work and fewer SS guards around, extended to the roads through the camp. On any other day, the road running between Camps C and D, which was the main access road for the B-II and B-III sectors, was busy with SS motorcycles and trucks driving back and forth, outside *Kommandos* marching to or from their work and groups of new arrivals making their way to the camps. On Sundays, however, there was very little of this traffic.

Women would sometimes gather behind the electric fence of Camp C, keeping a safe distance back, and talk to men gathered behind the Camp D fence on the other side of the road. They had to talk loudly – yell, really – as there was about 20 metres between them, but fathers and daughters, husbands and wives, brothers and sisters managed to reassure each other and communicate any news they may have heard about other family members or friends. Some took this further. They would write a note on a piece of paper, wrap it around a stone and throw it over the fences from one camp to the other. They threw other objects too, if they were a good enough weight to carry the distance.

I was worried that these people might be punished if an SS guard discovered they were communicating with each other – something that was strictly forbidden – so I positioned my *Läuferinnen* at various points along the fence to look out for any approaching SS and spread the word if necessary. Their warnings gave the prisoners along the fence time to 'disappear'.

My plan didn't work completely. I was doing my rounds one day when *Kommandant* Kramer appeared from nowhere. He told me he did not want the women and men to be talking to each other, and that in future on Sundays I should spend time walking up and down the road to make sure it wasn't happening.

Of course, this wasn't going to work as Kramer intended, and perhaps he knew that. I did as I was instructed, walking back and forth along the road for periods of time on Sundays. But before I started, I had my runners spread the word that when I was nearby, the women should fall back from the fence and stop talking or throwing items. Once I was past, however, I wouldn't see anything. Of course I couldn't possibly watch the whole of the road at any one moment.

Two or three weeks later I was on the road on a warm, sunny Sunday and noticed a motorcycle approaching. By the time it reached me, the men and women on both sides of the fence had retreated into their camps, leaving just myself and this SS officer in the middle of the road. When the motorcycle rider removed his goggles I realised it was *Kommandant* Kramer.

'Hellinger,' he said. 'What are you doing here?'

It seemed strange question, as he was the one who had given me this job. I thought perhaps he was having a joke, so I decided to play along.

'*Herr Lagerkommandant*, I was just thinking that I would like to go to the theatre,' I said with a half-smile. 'But I have nothing to wear. And I have no soap, no powder, no rouge, no lipstick and no perfume. And I have no brush for my hair. So I can't go to the theatre after all.'

Kramer thought for a moment.

To my astonishment, he said, 'You are right. You cannot go to the theatre looking like this. Tomorrow morning, I will pick you up and take you to get all the things you need.'

He then rode away.

When I returned to the camp, Gerda, Vera and Surka wanted to know why I was smiling. I told them about the joke I had shared with Kramer. We enjoyed a laugh and continued with our work, forgetting all about it.

The next morning, one of the *Läuferinnen* came running for me.

'*Lagerälteste*, please come to the front. *Lagerkommandant* Kramer is waiting for you.'

I could hardly believe this. I assumed perhaps Kramer wanted to see me for some other reason, so I approached him formally.

'*Dreiundzwanzig achtzehn* is reporting,' I said, clicking my heels as usual.

'Hellinger, we will go and get what you need for the theatre, as I promised.'

Thinking on my feet, I said, 'I will need some girls to come with me and help.'

'Bring them,' he said.

I turned to a runner and said, 'Quickly, gather fifty girls. The first fifty you can find, before he changes his mind.'

And so, a few minutes later the Birkenau commander Josef Kramer was walking with me towards the Kanada warehouse, with fifty girls following a short distance behind us.

When we reached the warehouse, after a walk of perhaps one-and-a-half kilometres, Kramer asked me to wait while he gathered the things I needed. As soon as he left, I told the girls behind me to hurry, collect a few trolleys and gather whatever they could from the Kanada blocks.

'Find soap, towels, blankets, jumpers, medicine. Anything that will be useful. Work quickly and pile it all onto the trolleys.' The trolleys were like large wooden wheelbarrows that could carry a lot of supplies. They were pulled from the front by one or two people.

The girls all ran off. In the meantime, I did as I had been told and waited. As I took in the scene I noticed that most of the buildings were overflowing with belongings. There had been so many new arrivals in recent weeks, there was just not enough space to store all their confiscated possessions.

After a little while I saw Kramer coming back towards me. He was carrying a small make-up console, the type that would sit on top of a dressing table. It had two drawers and a mirror on hinges that could be turned this way and that. Who knows how it had found its way to Birkenau. Over one arm was draped a long, black silk dress with what looked like a bright-red floral motif on the shoulder.

'In the drawers are soap, perfume, lipstick, a brush and comb, stockings and underwear. Now you can go to the theatre. Are you satisfied?'

'Yes,' I said. 'Very. Thank you very much. Everything is beautiful.'

Most beautiful, I thought, were the five overflowing trolleys the girls had by now queued up behind us.

'Please leave the console and the dress here,' I said to Kramer. 'The girls can help me carry them back to the camp.'

'No, I promised I would get it for you, so I will bring it,' he said.

And so we walked back to the camp, Kramer carrying the dress and the small table and never saying a word about the trolleys trundling along behind us – it was as if he was choosing to turn a blind eye to them. When we arrived back at the gate of Camp C, he put the console down and gave me the dress. He instructed the guard on the gate to let everything through, got back onto his motorcycle and rode away.

'Take everything to Block 2,' I told the girls with the trolleys. 'Take something for yourselves from this collection, then go and find all the doctors and bring them to me.'

Over the next day or so, the doctors took all the medicines and everything else was distributed between all the barracks, trying to ensure that as many women as possible got something. There would never be enough to provide more than a scrap of comfort to anyone, but there was enough to give many girls the tiniest glimpse back into their previous lives.

It was all the strangest situation. It was like finding an oasis in the desert. Was it a mirage? Did I dream it? I have sometimes wondered, but in the years since, others who were in the camp at that time have reminded me of it. It really happened.

The most interesting question is that of Kramer. How could someone like him, someone who would eventually be found guilty of the most terrible war crimes, who was responsible for the murder of thousands, also be so human? Did he see this whole exercise as some sort of sick joke at our expense, a moment of 'luxury' amidst our deprivation? Or was he seeking a sliver of normality himself? No one will ever know.

———

While Camp C was nearly always at its full capacity of 30,000, this was not a stable population. Women came and went all the time, sometimes in the hundreds. Just as selections took place after the arrival of each transport, they frequently took place inside the camps as well, led by the senior SS officers.

They looked for the sick or weak, sending them for *Sonderbehandlung* (SB), 'special treatment', one of a number of euphemisms the SS used for sending people to their deaths.

And they looked for people who had good eyesight and good hands, who were fit and well. They were transferred to other camps, such as the many sub-camps of Auschwitz that provided slave labour to German-owned factories. The largest of these was the Monowitz camp, also known as Auschwitz III, which provided workers to the large IG Farben rubber plant. Many of those who were able to do meaningful or specialist work for the Nazis would survive the war.

As *Lagerälteste* I had to stand beside the SS officer conducting the selection and watch impassively as young women, as healthy as they could be while living in hell, were sent to one side to await their fate. The girls themselves had no idea what was happening to them.

One of those who often performed selections on the ramp and inside the camps was Dr Josef Mengele, who came to be known as the 'Angel of Death'. He would select some prisoners for work, others for death and others to perform scientific experiments on. I was not aware of his pseudo-scientific work in the way I had been with the doctors in Block 10, but it would later be revealed that he carried out gruesome studies of twins, people who had eyes of different colours, and people with disabilities. Mengele was also enthusiastic about creating space in the *Revier* by sending everyone in the block for execution.

Mengele seemed to gain particular enjoyment from performing selections, often carrying out the task in an especially callous way. He would whistle the tune 'The Blue Danube' waltz as he made his selections, swinging a stick like a baton as if conducting an orchestra. On one beat he would send a girl to the right, to continue working, and on the next he would send another to the left, to the gas chambers. He usually showed no interest in whether someone was sick or well – his selections were random. He didn't care. His principle was the 'Final Solution': no Jews.

I was torn between wrenching sadness and burning anger during these selections, but I could show neither of these emotions.

After finishing his selection, Mengele would leave Camp C while a single guard led two columns of girls to the front of the camp: one group to be transported by truck to wherever they were needed as slave labour; the other to be taken to the gas chambers. The girls in this group did not know their fate, so there was no reason for them to resist, therefore the SS saw no need to use many guards.

One day my desperation overcame me and I seized a moment. I knew the numbers in each line had not yet been counted, so I stepped into the line selected for gassing and detached a group, saying, 'March with me. Don't ask any questions,' and steered the group of perhaps fifty girls silently back into the camp. I removed as many from the line as I thought I could get away with without anyone noticing. And they didn't – I got away with it. The action was so brazen and unexpected that nobody realised what was happening. I couldn't save everyone, but I could save a few, at least for another day.

The next time Mengele carried out a selection, he chose a larger number of young women for the gas chambers. I was furious. Again, after he had left and the line of girls had started moving to the front, I looked left and right to check for SS, stepped into the middle of the line and told a group to turn around and return to their barracks. This time I was able to take more, perhaps 100.

From then on I repeated this trick whenever I saw the chance. I observed the positions of the SS and camp leaders, and when I thought nobody was paying any attention, I stepped in and led some away. Sometimes it was only twenty, sometimes many more.

The SS were often coldly efficient, but there were flaws in their systems. One of the most glaring weaknesses was their arrogance: they could never imagine that a lowly, starving prisoner, even a *Lagerälteste*, would dare to be as brazen as I was.

Years later, in Israel, I would meet a lady named Chava, a survivor of Camp C, who told me of a time when many members of her extended family had been selected by Mengele.

'We all cried as they marched away,' she told me.

She said her younger cousin carefully followed the line towards the front. A few minutes later, she came running back, calling out, 'Don't cry! Magda is bringing them all back.'

Somehow, I had saved this lady's relatives. They were all so thankful. I, on the other hand, was thankful that it was only this young girl, and not an SS guard, who had seen me performing this dangerous trick.

Mengele seemed to have a special dislike for the younger women. During one selection he chose 800 girls no older than sixteen and ordered a guard to escort them to Block 3, which had been emptied a day or so before. He told the young SS guard to patrol and watch the doors, making sure no one came or went.

We knew this was a sure sign that these girls would be taken to the gas the next morning.

I spoke to Gerda. Was there anything we could do?

This time we decided to use another weakness in the SS's system: alcohol.

It's something of a myth that every SS guard was dedicated to the task and fundamentally evil. Of course, those who were dedicated and evil were the ones who rose through the ranks, but there were many more rank-and-file guards who were very bored most of their time. Many of them were often drunk or on drugs.

I remembered that there was a bottle of vodka in Block 30. A small *Kommando* regularly worked in that block repairing and maintaining sewing machines, and the German *Kapo* of this workgroup was very lazy. He didn't give a damn about getting any work done, or what his men were doing. Instead, he spent most of his time drunk, while the men under his command spent most of theirs talking. Overnight, he always stored his vodka in the room that would normally be used by a *Blockälteste*. Gerda and I knew where it was, so I asked her to go and get it. We didn't care if the *Kapo* missed it. His comfortable position depended on us turning a blind eye to his behaviour.

In the meantime I went to the young guard and chatted to him. He told me he was due to leave Birkenau the next day, as he was being deployed to fight on the Russian front. When Gerda joined us I shared the guard's story, and we made a big deal about how unlucky he was.

'We have some vodka,' Gerda said. 'Would you like a little?'

Of course, he agreed. He had a little, then a little bit more. Gerda kept talking to him and plying him with more drinks until finally, by around dusk, he fell into a drunken sleep.

As it got dark, I went to the back door of the block, banged on it and opened it.

'It's me, the *Lagerälteste*,' I called. 'I need a hundred girls to come with me right now.'

Walking in the usual ranks of five so as to look 'normal', I led the girls further into the camp. I went into a block, found the *Blockälteste* and told her she needed to accommodate these girls overnight.

'Don't ask any questions now,' I said. 'Just find a place for them. We'll sort it out tomorrow.'

I returned to Block 3 and took another hundred girls to another block, then repeated this process over and over until Block 3 was empty.

Gerda took the empty vodka bottle from the sleeping guard.

'Do you know anything about this?' I asked.

She shook her head.

'So you don't know, and I don't know. Let's go and get some sleep,' I said.

The next morning the guard was gone and, of course, Block 3 was empty. We soon had all the girls back in their original blocks, as though Mengele's selection had never happened. To our amazement, the 'disappearance' of these 800 girls was never mentioned, though who knows what happened to the guard. It didn't matter. Thanks to Gerda and me and a bottle of alcohol, those 800 girls lived to see another day.

Another time one of the *Stubendienster*, Irene, came into Block 2 to find me. She cried as she told me she'd received news that Mengele had selected a group of boys – teenagers – to be sent to the gas chambers the next day. Two of the group were her sister's beautiful sons.

'A male prisoner told me he might be able to save my nephews if I could find him a wrist watch – a Schaffhausen watch,' Irene told me. No doubt he had plans to use this watch to his own advantage at some point, perhaps to save his own life. Valuable items like this were the illicit currency of the camp.

I had a runner deliver a message to someone I knew who worked in Kanada. There were thousands of confiscated watches in there, and this person had the job of sorting them so the Nazis could sell them. I never knew the details of how it happened, but somehow the desired watch was found and smuggled to the man who had asked for it. The two boys were rescued. Sadly, the remainder were sent up the chimneys.

When I received news that a very close family friend, Erich Kulka, had arrived at Camp D, I immediately made arrangements to visit him. Erich was always well connected, and after we had greeted each other he said he needed to pass on some news.

'News has travelled,' he said. 'The underground have been aware of your work and they hold you in very high esteem.'

He placed a ring in my hand. It featured a prominent symbol that looked like the letters 'P' and 'W'.

'They want you to have this ring. It was the type of ring worn by the resistance during the Warsaw ghetto uprising in 1943.'

From then on, I wore the ring as much as I could, only removing it when I thought it might bring trouble. I felt very proud of it, especially because someone had taken such a significant risk to smuggle it into the camp in the first place. I thought wearing it was also the safest place for it – if it was on my finger it was less likely to get lost.

However, there was one time when it nearly cost me my life.

A runner arrived one morning with the message that I was to go to the front of the camp immediately. When I got there, I found Grese and Mengele standing near the guard's hut. Just at that moment, Kramer's large black limousine drove through the gate.

The car came to a stop in front of me. Sitting in the back seat on the far side, Kramer called to me through the open window.

'Hellinger. I want to inspect the camp. Get in.'

This created a dilemma. I had to obey Kramer's order, but I was very conscious that Grese and Mengele were beside me, and it was not in my interests to embarrass them.

'*Herr Kommandant*, how will it look if a Jewess is sitting next to the *Lagerkommandant*? Please take Dr Mengele in the car with you. I can walk.'

'Let him walk!' he yelled. 'You will sit in the car.'

I thought perhaps I should not object any further, but then noticed the running board – the step that ran along the bottom of the doors of luxury cars in those days.

'I will stand on the running board,' I said.

'Alright, stand on the step,' he said.

I stepped onto the board and took hold of the door to steady myself. At that moment, Kramer's face reddened.

His voice low, he said, 'What do you have on your finger?'

I dropped my eyes in shock. I had forgotten to remove the ring!

'You dare to wear the ring of the uprising on your finger?' Kramer pulled the handgun from his belt and held it towards my hand, just inches away.

'I'm going to shoot your finger off right now.'

I didn't move, but held my breath, waiting for him to shoot.

He looked at me.

'Why don't you move your hand?'

'Whether I move it or not, if you want to shoot my finger you will,' I said.

'Now I will shoot your whole hand off,' he said.

Still, I kept my hand in place.

'I'm sorry I wore this ring,' I said. 'I won't anymore.'

Kramer stared at me for a long moment, then relaxed his grip and returned the gun to its holster.

'Get in the car,' he said, and this time I complied without objection. I dared not look at Grese and Mengele after this exchange, but I was well aware that Kramer had raised my stature in their eyes, whether he meant to or not. Perhaps he was just trying to taunt Mengele; it was well known the two men loathed each other.

Kramer and I drove some way into the camp then walked around inspecting some barracks, the washrooms and the latrines.

'You are keeping everything in good order, as you promised,' he said finally.

I was pleased to report to my staff that their efforts had succeeded in keeping the SS at bay.

And from then on, I was more careful about when I wore my ring.

———

One of the most boring jobs in the camps on Sunday afternoons was that of the SS guard at the camp gate. With almost no one coming or going, he usually spent this time in his hut getting very drunk. On one occasion – I think it was in around September 1944 – this guard sent a runner to find me.

When I arrived he was already slurring his speech, and wobbly on his feet.

'Do you have a boyfriend?' he asked.

'No, I don't,' I said.

'Why not? You should have a boyfriend.'

'Nobody wants me,' I said. *How would I have time for a boyfriend anyway?* I thought to myself. It was absurd.

In his intoxicated state, the guard was upset by my reply.

'The first man who passes by here has to want you,' he said. 'You wait and see.'

A few minutes later, the long line of a large male *Kommando* approached Camp C on the road outside the camp. They were marching back to Camp D.

'You! Come here and talk to this woman,' the guard called to one of the men at the front of the line.

The man came over as instructed. He stood there a moment, then asked me my name.

'Magda,' I replied.

'And where are you from?'

'I . . . I can't do this,' I said. 'Making small talk with a stranger I just met on the street.' I turned to the guard. 'And besides, this man has duties.'

'You are right,' said the guard. Addressing the man, he said, 'Tomorrow morning you will report to this gate.'

Then he turned to me. 'You will be here as well, and make sure you write his number in the book.' He was referring to the register of people who came and went from the camp.

When I returned to Block 2, Gerda and Surka asked what had happened. They laughed and teased me when they heard the story, wondering what would happen the next day.

The next morning I returned to the front gate as instructed. After a short time the man from the previous day arrived. He wrote his number in the book: 65066. Then he came inside the hut. He handed the guard a bottle of schnapps he had organised, and the guard went away.

I suddenly felt very embarrassed. I don't really know why, but I ran away, saying I had work to do. I ran right to the back of the camp and into Block 30, and hid there.

After a while it was my little cousin Aliska who found me. She was only fourteen, but she gave me a lecture. 'You don't have to marry him. Just talk to him a little.'

Later on – I don't remember if it was that same day or a bit later – the man returned to try to speak to me again. This time he took the risk to come into my room in Block 2. I introduced myself again and finally learned his name, Béla. Feeling nervous, I turned away and looked into a small mirror I had on the wall. I picked up a comb and tried to tidy my hair.

'It's been a long time since I saw a woman comb her hair,' he said.

I turned around and for the first time noticed that he looked quite handsome, with the bluest blue eyes. I suddenly felt closer to him. Nevertheless, if someone had told me at the time that standing there was the man I would marry and spend the rest of my life with, I would have called them insane.

Over the next few weeks Béla was able to organise permission to visit Camp C, which gave him the chance to visit me. We never did anything more than talk. We both knew that to get too close to each other would be risky. It was hard enough to negotiate survival in this place without falling into the trap of a complicated, dangerous relationship.

Grese saw him a few times. Teasing us, she would sing a German song to him: 'The whole world is blue / as the sky / when I look into your eyes'. She seemed to approve, and tolerated his coming and going.

A little later on I managed to organise a job for Béla with the small *Kommando* that worked on the sewing machines in Block 30 – the one with the perpetually drunk *Kapo*. This was one thing I could do to make Béla's life easier. We didn't see a lot of each other – I was too busy, and maintaining order remained my main priority. But we did see each other from time to time.

11

Béla's story

In the small amounts of time we had together, Béla shared some of his story with me.

Béla Blau was six years older than me, born in 1910 in the city known today as Bratislava, on the Danube River. He was the eighth child in a Jewish family, and told me about having the job, from the age of just five, of queuing for bread and milk at five in the morning. His schooling was conducted in both German and Hungarian, which became useful when at sixteen he started an apprenticeship as a salesman in a textile business.

Béla married in 1937 and he and his wife, Irma, moved to the smaller city of Žilina. They had a son, Ervin, later that year. By then Béla had worked for the photographic company Agfa for a number of years, but in 1938 he was dismissed because of his Jewish background. Some time later, he and his family, including his mother-in-law, who was living with them, were thrown out of their centrally located apartment by the Hlinka Guard as part of the new Slovak government's policy of Aryanisation. They were forced to the outer edge of the city. This was really when the war started for Béla.

'Day-to-day life was full of fear and tension,' Béla told me. 'The Hlinka Guard were taking people away at any time, so every time we heard someone go past the front of our house, we worried there would be a knock on our door.'

He did whatever work he could to feed his family until sometime in 1941, when the guards did come to the door. They took Béla and his family to a nearby concentration camp – it may have been a transit camp – where they naturally thought they might be imprisoned or killed. Béla never knew the reason, but after only a few days they were released and sent home, though without most of their belongings.

'One day after Yom Kippur in 1942,' Béla told me, 'it was around 21 September, there was another knock on our door. There were two men in civilian clothing and two others in the Hlinka Guard uniform carrying guns. I knew one of the civilians – he was a local man – but he would not acknowledge me. They told us we had thirty minutes to collect our belongings and then ordered us – me, my five-year-old son, my wife and her mother – to follow them.

'We were taken to the transit camp again, but this time instead of going into the camp, the man I knew told us to wait outside the office with a group of about thirty others. Inside I could hear some sort of commotion – people seemed to be arguing about something. After a while, the man came out with a bundle of papers and instructed us to go with him. We walked some way along the length of a cattle train, and as we passed one with the door still open noticed it was crammed full of people. I thought I recognised the terrified people inside speaking French, but as we walked past more wagons I heard screaming in other languages – Polish, and some other languages I didn't recognise.

'Finally, this man instructed me, my family and the rest of the group to board an empty wagon. Just before I went up – because I knew this man – I asked him to let me see the paper in his hand.

'"Give it to me," I said.

'He handed me the paper and I saw forty names on it, all typed out. Four of the typed names had been crossed out and my name and those of my family had been added in pencil. We weren't meant to be on this train; someone had bribed their way off it and we were their replacements.'

Béla told me that this corrupt official and others like him would eventually end up in Auschwitz themselves. They were recognised by other inmates who, like Béla and his family, had been substituted on the transport lists in return for bribes. Some of these treacherous men were killed by the inmates they had betrayed; thrown against the electric fences or beaten up.

Béla and his family travelled in their cattle wagon uncomfortably, though not squeezed in tight like those in the other cars. They arrived at Auschwitz main camp after a couple of nights.

By now the SS had started the selections on the ramp. As usual, women with children and older people went one way, men and women who were able to work went the other. Béla was separated from the rest of his family.

With tears in his eyes, he told me he had not objected. None of them knew what was ahead of them. It was only sometime later that he learnt the terrible truth: that his young son, his wife and her mother would all have been gassed, then buried in a mass grave behind the camp.

_____

Béla and the other *Zwangarbeiter*, forced labourers, were processed in the sauna, all their belongings and clothes removed from them.

'I was given a pair of striped pants and a striped shirt that was two sizes too small. It would take a few weeks before I had lost enough weight to fit into it. For some reason we were allowed to keep our shoes, which I held between my knees as I put the shirt on. However, a Polish prisoner who was working in the sauna pushed me so I lost my balance, picked up my shoes and ran away with them.'

Somehow Béla had also managed to keep his wristwatch, which he later exchanged with a prisoner who worked in the *Politische Abteilung*, the political department, in return for a pair of shoes.

At first Béla was in Block 10 – the same block that would later become the experimental block for women, where I would be the *Blockälteste*. It was a shock to him to peer through the small cracks in the window shutters and see executions taking place against the wall between Blocks 10 and 11.

He got an even bigger shock a few days later, when one of his friends went out to work on a *Kommando* one day and they brought him home dead. 'The men who carried him told me that the Polish *Vorarbeiter*, foreman, had told my friend, "Listen, if you promise me that you'll give me your ration in the evening then I will leave you alone." My friend refused – he still had a little courage – and this made the *Vorarbeiter* angry. He hit my friend with a spade and killed him. As a prisoner himself, this was insubordination by the *Vorarbeiter*, and so he was later beaten to death himself by a group of German prisoners.'

Béla told me that they were constantly harassed in those first days in the camp.

'They would wake us at midnight and force us outside for *Zählappell* for no reason whatsoever. Other times they chased us down the stairs to the front of the building. We would have to stand for hours next to our beds. Anyone caught inside during the day, no matter how sick or weak, would be sent to Block 11 for punishment, or to the gas chambers on the next transport.'

Béla worked in a number of different *Kommandos* himself. He scraped the bark from trees with a spade as part of a bridge building project, then he worked on building the Union munitions factory. The *Kapo* on this project was illiterate, and because Béla spoke perfect German, the *Kapo* had Béla do writing jobs for him. In return, he organised clean clothes for Béla. These clothes may have saved his life. By then Béla was quite weak from lack of food, and during an unexpected selection in the camp in around January 1943, he was worried that he might be sent left, to the gas chambers. But the SS officer thought he looked quite good and sent him right. It turned out those sent right were moved to work in the Kanada warehouse at Birkenau, which was a much safer job than the outside *Kommandos*.

'We were sorting all the effects from the people who came on the transports – sorting it all out to be sent to Germany.'

Béla was working with the small items: spectacles, cutlery, shaving brushes . . . these sorts of things. He had to pack them into cane baskets, close them up and write a card that said 'KL Au', for *Konzentrationslager Auschwitz*, and listed the items in the basket. There were hundreds and hundreds of these baskets.

Working in Kanada had benefits not only because it was safer, with fewer beatings and better working conditions, but also because it was possible, if you were careful, to take some clean underwear for warmth, or to find food that had been left in people's suitcases. The food provided extra strength, or it could be shared with friends or used for favours.

In around April 1943, Béla contracted typhus. This was dangerous. At the time, his accommodation block was at the Auschwitz main camp, three kilometres away from his work in Birkenau. The weather was hot, and while walking that distance he would likely have collapsed, which was almost certainly a sentence to go up the chimney. He went to the *Revier* at Auschwitz main camp, where it turned out there were very few patients. A friend of his told him that it had recently been cleared out, so it was safe for Béla to rest there for a few days before it filled up again. He got out with just a day or two to spare.

When Béla had a toothache a little later, he went to another friend who was a dentist to have the tooth pulled out. To say thank you, Béla smuggled a cigarette out of Kanada, but on that day his work group were strip searched, and the cigarette was discovered. Béla was sentenced to two months working in the *Strafkommando*, punishment brigade.

'It was very hard. We were digging channels to drain water in a swampy area. We were working up to our waists in mud and had to pull each other out at the end of the day.'

After this time Béla managed to find some more clerical work, which made his life a little bit easier. A friend got him a job back in Kanada, but then he was subject to some jealousy from other prisoners.

'One day, one of the fellows said to me, "When you come tomorrow, you will not be going home." I didn't go there anymore.'

Around that time, a new *Kommando* started up that involved dismantling aircraft that had been shot down in the area around Auschwitz.

'They were of all different types: German, British and American. We would strip the aluminium and other useful materials from the planes, which then went to German factories to be recycled.

'I befriended that *Kapo* too, helping him with the writing. That was how I became the *Schreiber* for the *Kommando*. This job became quite big, because the group built up to about 1300 men and twenty-six *Kapo*. I had to keep an accurate record of every single one. There was a situation where two Russian prisoners tried to escape. I was called to the front, where the SS asked me what the numbers of these two prisoners were. I turned to go back and get my papers, and saw my assistant running towards me waving the papers in the air. We gave them to the SS and they sent us away. I don't know whether the Russians were ever caught, but I know that if I hadn't been able to provide the numbers, both me and my assistant probably would have been sent to the gas.

'There was something I was able to do in this job to make life easier for the other prisoners, but it was risky. The aircraft wreckage used to arrive from the surrounding areas on trains, and we would need to go to the railway tracks to unload it onto trucks. These were the same sections of track where the transports of new prisoners stopped for disembarking. Sometimes we would have to wait for our train while a new transport was unloaded.

'At the end of the ramp was a small signalman's hut that was always empty, so at these times I would go and hide in that hut and watch the unloading of the transport from afar. I could see the many Kanada workers whose job it was, after the selection, to collect the belongings of the new arrivals and put them on trucks to move to the warehouse for sorting. These workers had become very skilled at finding any food amongst these belongings and hiding it. One of the workers was a friend of mine whose name was Ferdo. After the ramp was empty again, Ferdo would come to the hut and share his collection of food with me.

'One day Ferdo shared quite a good harvest with me. I took this back to our *Kommando* and called all the twenty-six *Kapo* together. I told them, "Listen. Give me the sticks that you are using to beat people." They were very surprised by this. "I will give you food in return. I have all the raw ingredients and I need your sticks to make a small fire and cook something for you to eat."

'And so, amazingly, they gave up their sticks. In my mind if I saved only two or three beatings each day it would be worth it, but from then on I continued with this game and slowly, slowly, the beating let up. They kept screaming at people, of course, but screaming doesn't hurt anybody.'

'Another of my jobs was to arrange all 1300 men into rows of five for the four-kilometre march back to our camp at the end of the day. One Sunday I was leading them past Camp C and there was a drunken guard at the front. He called me over and pointed to a pretty woman, and he told me to talk to her.'

Béla told me that as soon as he learnt my name, he went to his close friend, Erich Kulka, knowing that Erich often worked in Camp C. 'Listen, Erich, what is your opinion about Magda? Do you know her?'

'Yes, I know her very well,' Erich said. 'I will tell you my opinion in one sentence. She is one of the few people here in the camp who manages to still be human.'

After telling me all this, Béla looked at me with a grin.

'Since then, I've come to Camp C whenever I could get permission.'

12

Resistance

July 1944

The dislike and jealousy amongst the SS came to the surface again after Birkenau sector B-IIb was liquidated.

I had nothing to do with that camp, but I knew it as the Theresienstadt family camp – a camp that was dedicated to housing Jewish families from a ghetto in the town of Theresienstadt in Czechoslovakia. Most of the first 7000 prisoners in the camp, including many children, had been gassed during a first liquidation in March 1944. Since then, another 7000 prisoners had arrived, but now, in July 1944, they, too, had been murdered.

The *Lagerführerin* of that camp was a terrible, vicious SS guard called Luise Danz. Unwilling to lose her position because of the closure of her camp, she somehow used her influence to push Grese out of her role and take over as *Lagerführerin* of Camp C. She then came to me.

'You will no longer be *Lagerälteste* here. I will use my *Lageräl-teste* from B-IIb and my other functionaries in other positions.'

I thought she probably expected me to object, but I wasn't going to give her that pleasure. There was nothing I could do anyway, so I said nothing. I became *Blockälteste* of Block 26, while Gerda and Surka, who were also pushed out, also found other positions.

It was soon clear that things would change if Danz remained in charge. There was no longer any interest in cleanliness. After rain storms the ground became very muddy. We kept Block 26 as clean as we could, but there was mud all over the rest of the camp, inside and out. There was also more violence in the camp, if that was possible. Like Grese, Danz carried a whip. However, rather than using hers in bursts of temper as Grese did, Danz used her whip all the time, striking left and right just to get women to return to their barracks.

Block 26 was close to Block 30, where the drunk *Kapo* had his *Kommando*. I now discovered he was good for something: he had been at Auschwitz for a long time, and so was well connected.

He came to me after hearing about my replacement by Danz from a young *Blockälteste*. He had been speaking to other guards, and told me that I shouldn't worry, because in two or three days both Grese and I would be reinstated to our positions. And so it was. A couple of days later, Grese returned. She reappointed me as *Lagerälteste*, and we put Gerda and Surka back into their positions.

The SS liked to think they were in total control of the camps, but as this *Kapo*'s intervention demonstrated, they never had it entirely their own way.

Occasionally there were brave instances of individual resistance, though sadly these almost always failed. One day an SS guard started striking out at everyone nearby. A small Greek girl decided she had had enough, so she started to hit him like a boxer. We knew her as a singer, as she used to sing 'Mamma son tanto felice' to us. We learnt later that she was also a trained boxer. She was hitting him powerfully, left and right. However, the SS man was large and her blows did not have much effect. He grabbed her by the neck and started to throw her against a barrel. He thrashed her until she was dead. We were proud of her daring, but very sorry she had paid for it with her life.

More subtle, and successful, resistance came from those of us who had a little more leeway because of our positions, and so were able to find ways to resist or circumvent the Nazis' control.

I've already described some of the ways I was able to do this, whether by 'organising' extra food or belongings through contacts in the kitchens or Kanada, hiding the unwell during roll calls, manipulating Grese by identifying her weaknesses and so on.

Something else we could do was influence the transfer of some prisoners to factories. Many years after the war I received a letter from a survivor named Yolli Frank, who reminded me of how I had been able to save her family by organising their transfer to a factory away from Auschwitz. After arriving at Birkenau in June 1944, Yolli discovered that my name was Hellinger. She introduced herself to me, as she had Hellinger relatives herself, and we discovered we were cousins. Initially I was able to organise for Yolli and her sister Lili to work in the camp kitchen. Then I heard that a transport was to take a group of prisoners to the Siemens factory in Nuremberg.

I knew from the girls who performed clerical roles in the main office that this factory was a safer place to be than Birkenau. Of the many factories that requested labourers from the Auschwitz–Birkenau camps, the girls could deduce which were the most dangerous from the number of prisoners each factory requested. All of these factories were using prisoners as slave labour, but some took better care of their workers than others. It seemed likely that those making regular requests for large numbers of prisoners were replacing inmates who had died through starvation or abuse, so we saw these facilities as high risk and to be avoided. Other factories – Siemens was one of them – rarely requested replacement staff, so they were considered safer. Of course, we had reports on these factories through our networks as well.

Working secretly with the clerical girls, I was able to put Yolli and Lili's names on the transport list for Siemens. They ended up working there in the kitchens, and survived the war.

I was able to have others transferred to the Krupp munitions factory in Silesia, where they were able to live in much safer conditions.

I wasn't the only one able to manipulate these lists. People like Katja, in her role as *Rapportschreiberin*, and others in senior functionary positions could also do so. And of course, our influence was limited. The clerks always had to provide the requested number of prisoners, even to the dangerous factories, so we couldn't save everyone.

There were many other forms of small, passive resistance that most of the long-term prisoners used whenever they could. We told new arrivals about how the camps worked and what they could do to improve their chances of survival. We warned them who the most dangerous SS officers and guards were. We shared little pieces of news, such as letting a woman know that her husband or son had been confirmed as being alive. Prisoners who worked with civilians in some of the nearby factories sometimes brought back snippets of news of what was happening in the outside world.

And we worked together. I constantly encouraged women to work together, as this was a very simple form of resistance. A lonely, isolated woman was always more vulnerable than one who had others looking out for her.

There were also other larger-scale forms of resistance going on around me.

Secret resistance groups formed based on nationality and background. There were groups of Polish, German or Austrian political prisoners, and others of Slovak, Czech or Polish Jewish men, along with various groups of women. Sometimes these groups worked together, with members holding clandestine meetings on Sundays or German holidays, when there were fewer SS around. They would coordinate plans for sabotage, for escape attempts, for smuggling medicines or other supplies or for trying to get information out into the wider world. Another form of resistance was making copies of documents, which were then buried in the grounds around the camp. These were intended to provide evidence after the war, in the event that the Nazis destroyed all their own documentation.

We often heard stories of sabotage by workers to reduce the efficiency of the German factories. Béla once told me how the men he was working with to dismantle damaged aircraft would make sure to cripple any instrumentation or other parts that might otherwise have been reused. The most famous attempt at sabotage would occur in October 1944, when members of the *Sonderkommando*, the prisoners who were forced to manage and empty the crematoriums, blew up crematorium IV. We knew nothing about this until we heard a huge explosion in the middle of the day. Unfortunately, no one who took part in that rebellion survived, and the SS still had three other facilities to continue their exterminations.

None of us could prevent the worst of what the SS were aiming to do, especially the mass murder of people immediately after their transports arrived. All we could do was try to slow the Nazi machine and possibly save a life here and there, even if only for a day.

The ultimate form of resistance would have been escape. Everybody talked about escaping all the time, though few were serious about it. There were always whispers about prisoners planning to escape, or actually doing so. One day a man called David came into our camp to do maintenance work on a roof. I knew he was a member of the camp resistance so wondered whether, he would include us in any uprising or escape plans if we did favours for him such as organising food. I passed food up to where he was working through a little window in the roof so that nobody would see. When Erich Kulka and another resistance member, Otto Kraus, came together to repair a broken door, I helped them in a similar way. However, nothing came of any of this. At one point, David did suggest we should escape together. He said he had connections, but he had no clear plan. And when I thought about it, I decided I didn't want to leave behind all the women who depended on me. I said no to David, and prayed the war would end soon.

While we all dreamed of escape, we also knew it was extremely risky with a very low chance of success.

———

Every form of resistance had to be conducted very carefully to avoid attracting the attention of informers.

The *Politische Abteilung*, the political department, was effectively the Gestapo, or secret police, for the camp. It ran a network of informants, mostly German prisoners, in opposition to the underground. There was a lovely Polish girl who worked in the *Politische Abteilung*. This gave her a little extra freedom, which she used to plan an escape with her Polish boyfriend. Sadly, one of them must have made a mistake because people started following them. Soon after, her boyfriend was quietly 'disappeared', and the girl was arrested and interrogated by the SS. To ensure that we all got the message, her violent interrogation was made into a show, taking place in the open in Camp C, with everyone required to watch. After the SS had had enough, they broke her hands and feet and finally hanged her. They left her hanging for a day before she was thrown onto a trolley and disposed of in the crematorium.

I'd had my own experience with the *Politische Abteilung* when I was summoned to the department around August 1944. I had no idea why they wanted to see me, but I didn't expect good news. The department was responsible for most of the camp record keeping, including tracking the arrival and departure (by whatever means) of prisoners. But most of us knew of it for its role as the camp's police force and intelligence department, trying to prevent dissent or uprisings. I wondered whether they had discovered a conversation I'd had with one of the members of the underground. Or had they found out about my activities organising food or medicines?

I walked into the interrogation room, where I found *SS-Hauptsturmführer* Wilhelm Boger, yet another SS officer with a reputation for extreme barbarism, and two other SS who I didn't recognise.

The men started questioning me about any relatives of mine in Palestine and any contact I'd had with people outside the camp. They asked about any letters or postcards I had written. They wanted to know how people in Palestine would have known I was in Auschwitz. I had no idea. The men were very rough, pushing me to give them the answers they were looking for, but as I had no idea why they were questioning me, it was hard to give them what they wanted.

Finally, I was ordered to sign some papers, though again I didn't know why. They pushed me out the door. It was obvious something was worrying them.

Over the next few days, I came across a few other women who had also been questioned in this way. We were all Slovakians who had been on the first transports in 1942, and we worked out that some of us, though not all, had been members of the Hashomer Hatzair youth organisation. All of us had functionary roles, whether in the camps or in the offices, which gave us enough freedom that we were able to write occasional letters back to relatives and friends in our home towns. But that was all we could work out.

It wouldn't be until long after the war that this mystery would be solved by a Slovakian historian, Yehoshua Büchler, who was an Auschwitz survivor himself. In 2002, in the journal *Yad Vashem Studies*, he told the amazing story of an improbable attempt to rescue forty-one inmates of Auschwitz–Birkenau and two other concentration camps.

From soon after the first transport left Slovakia, many Jewish individuals and organisations, including activist organisations like Hashomer Hatzair, started making efforts to find out where people like myself and, later, my family were being taken and what was happening to them. They continued in these efforts throughout the war. By talking to those who worked on the rail networks, they calculated movement of transport trains. They used information from letters and postcards sent from inside ghettos and camps, and reports from various underground members and from the small number of people who managed to escape. These people and organisations tried to prevent people being deported by helping them escape to other countries or by providing them with paperwork to prove that they were citizens of another country. Some Slovakian Jews avoided deportation, or were able to escape from ghettos, after obtaining immigration visas to Palestine.

Inside the camps, however, we knew very little about all this.

In early 1944, two members of the Jewish underground in Slovakia, Yaakov Rosenberg and Moshe Weiss, escaped Europe and made their way to Palestine. There, they gave a list of names to the Yishuv leadership (the leadership of the Jewish population in Palestine) and the Jewish Agency Immigration Department. The names were of Slovakians who they believed, based on letters and postcards, were being held at Auschwitz–Birkenau and two other concentration camps.

I was on that list. The details on the list included the tattoo numbers of some of us, and for others it showed the block numbers where we were believed to be living.

Rosenberg and Weiss knew they had to act quickly. They knew the people on their list were among the last of the thousands of Slovakians who had been deported in 1942, and hoped that if we could be granted a foreign nationality, including visas, we might be released from the camps. They asked the Jewish Agency to issue 'certificates' to the people on the list – certificates that would act as immigration visas to Palestine.

Initially, Rosenberg and Weiss were not taken seriously. However, in June 1944, the Jewish leadership heard from two Auschwitz escapees, Rudolf Vrba and Alfred Wetzler, who had managed to return to Slovakia. Finally, the reality that Auschwitz was a camp for mass extermination started to be understood and taken seriously in the outside world.

In August 1944, certificates were issued in the names of twenty Auschwitz prisoners. A letter from Rosenberg to the Palestine mission in Geneva lists those of us who were allocated certificates, including the certificate number and, where it was known, the person's block number and/or tattoo number. My certificate is listed as number M/438/43/Yh/30.

The names and details of twenty-one other prisoners from Auschwitz and Theresienstadt are also included in Rosenberg's letter, but without certificate numbers. The Palestine office addressed individual letters to each person on the list, and the list itself was forwarded to the German authorities to be 'processed'.

Those letters apparently did reach the offices of the camp, and were then passed on to the *Politische Abteilung*, where they would have been inspected by censors. The Nazis were apparently quite concerned about how anyone outside Auschwitz knew the names of any of their prisoners, let alone our tattoo numbers or block numbers. Of course, they never passed the letters on to us, but in a bizarre German effort to stick to the rules, they had us sign documents to show that (though we didn't know it) the letters had been received.

———

Over the three months before August 1944, trains arrived almost daily at Birkenau, sometimes multiple times a day, carrying thousands and thousands of Hungarians. In Camp C we were too far away to see what was going on, though if I went to the back of the camp I might see streams of newly arrived women, children and the elderly being led towards the gas chambers. A much smaller number of men and women from each transport were marched to camps that had the capacity to accommodate them, including Camp C.

These transports stopped at around the time when the Theresienstadt family camp was liquidated. After that, the number of new arrivals at Birkenau slowed.

We started to wonder if this meant things were changing in the war. One of the more common rumours was that the Russians were pushing the Germans back on the eastern front. Some were saying that the war would soon be over, but those of us who had survived almost three years in this hell did not allow ourselves to believe that. 'Soon' may never come.

Even though the number of new arrivals slowed, the SS still needed many prisoners as labourers, so Camp C continued to house nearly 30,000 women. That changed from September, when a wave of selections took place. Many prisoners were sent away to other labour camps in the Nazis' network; those who were sick or unwell were sent up the chimneys. The rest were spread around other camps within Birkenau, including some to sector B-Ib, next to sector B-Ia where I had started my life at Birkenau nearly two years before. Grese also moved away from Camp C, though I didn't know where.

Around this time there also seemed to be an increase in activity. We noticed trains and trucks being loaded with large quantities of materials, including goods from the Kanada warehouse, to be shipped away, presumably into Germany.

Were the Germans worried that they were losing the war?

Eventually, seemingly without warning, I was *Lagerälteste* of an empty camp.

At first I wondered if the Nazis were planning to bring in thousands of new inmates to fill Camp C again. But soon after, Kramer came to see me.

'Hellinger, come with me,' he said. 'You are not *Lagerälteste* anymore. I am going to take you somewhere where you will need to work harder.'

'I can work as hard as any other Jewish woman,' I replied.

'Oh, but you don't know how hard,' he said. He seemed to be turning this conversation into some sort of game.

'I'm nothing special,' I said.

He took me to the kitchen block in sector B-Ib, where he announced to Schultz, the SS woman in charge, 'Here is Magda. She will be the new leader of the women in the kitchen.'

So my job would be to manage everything in the kitchen. But there was a problem. I knew that the current leader in this kitchen, whose name was Franzi, was the girlfriend of the camp's *Lagerälteste*. This *Lagerälteste* was a German political prisoner who had always been very good to the Jewish girls, so I had no reason to make her unhappy or make an enemy of her. If I replaced Franzi as leader, what would happen to her?

After Kramer had left, I said to Schultz, 'I have no idea how to manage a kitchen, and Franzi is already doing a very good job. I would rather do work in the office. I can do the counting work, calculating the amounts of supplies we need.'

Schultz looked doubtful.

'But what will *Lagerkommandant* Kramer say? He told me you were to be the leader.'

'He will be satisfied,' I said, bluffing. I was fairly sure Kramer would never know.

'Okay,' said Schultz, 'you will do the counting in the office.'

A few days later a girl called Regina came to see me. She had worked in the kitchen at Camp C but did not have a secure job in camp B-Ib, which always meant there was a risk of being selected out. She asked for my help.

I went to Schultz. 'There is so much work in the counting. Can I have a helper?'

She shrugged. 'Have as many as you need,' she said.

'One will do,' I said.

Regina and I worked well together, making a few 'mistakes' in the counting here and there so that everyone in the camp got a little more food.

After all the worry and constant fear that came with being *Lagerälteste*, I was very comfortable in this new office job.

It was a bit of a rest. For this short time I was separated from the ongoing pain and brutality of daily life in the camp, protected from *Zählappell*, shielded from the burden of trying to minimise harm and save lives.

But it was only a short time.

Only two or three weeks after I moved to the kitchen, a *Läuferin* came into the office.

'Magda Hellinger to the front!' she called.

When a prisoner without a senior functionary role (as I was now) was called to the front, it was often a bad sign. It might mean you were going to the *Politische Abteilung*, suspected of some type of underground activity. Many did not return from such a call. I had no particular fear, because I had been called to the front many times as *Lagerälteste*. But many of the girls were worried, some kissing and hugging me goodbye as I walked.

As I approached the camp gate, I recognised *SS-Hauptsturmführer* Kramer's black car waiting for me once again.

'Hellinger,' he said as I drew near. 'Sit in the car.'

As we started to drive, Kramer looked at me and said, *'Was haben Sie ausgefressen?'* which roughly means: 'What have you been up to?' or 'What trouble have you made?'

I answered simply that I always did the best I could for the people and for the running of the camp.

We drove down the straight road between sectors B-IIc (Camp C) and B-IId (Camp D), and as we did so he asked me that same question a number of times. *'Was haben Sie ausgefressen?'*

I quietly gave the same answer each time, becoming increasingly concerned that Kramer had discovered some sort of 'crime'

I had committed. I thought of some letters I had left in my room at Camp C – letters for the men's camp that I had never had the opportunity to deliver. Or had I left some 'organised' belongings in that room?

'*Was haben Sie ausgefressen?*'

'I always did the best I could for the people and for the running of the camp,' I repeated.

As we approached the end of the road, my chest tightened. A right turn would point the car towards Camp C and the administration buildings. But a left turn would take us towards the gas chambers.

Was I being personally escorted to my end by the camp *Kommandant*?

'*Was haben Sie ausgefressen?*'

And then the car turned right, into Camp C.

'Get out of the car,' said Kramer.

As we stood near the entrance of the camp, he said, 'You say you always did your best for the camp and for the people. So now I am making you *Lagerälteste* of Camp C once more. However, this time the camp will be a working camp. There will be *Weberei*, weaving mills, in here.'

And so I became *Lagerälteste* again. And once again I brought some of the other Slovakian girls with me, including Gerda, to act as *Blockältesten* and other assistant roles. However, it wasn't like before. There was only a relatively small number of prisoners in the camp this time, who mostly worked on the weaving, making products needed for the German war effort.

There was one advantage of being back at Camp C. Over in Block 30, Béla was still working with the always-drunk *Kapo* in the *Kommando* repairing sewing machines. Now we could see each other again sometimes.

One evening he stepped out of the *Kommando* before they marched back to their camp. He came up to me and said, 'Magda, I want to marry you.'

'Don't you see the chimneys?' I said. 'There is no life here, let alone marriage.'

'I mean after the war,' he replied.

'But you are a travelling salesman. I would never marry a traveller who is away all week and only home on the weekend.'

His head dropped a little, and he rejoined his group.

Another time he asked to talk to me in my room, but an SS guard spotted him and screamed, 'You have no right to be here!' Béla quickly moved away.

A while later there was a small fire in the weaving room and Béla joined some other men to help put it out. After they had succeeded, he came into my room. Once again, he told me that he wanted to marry me after the war. I don't know if I said yes – I was too afraid of the uncertainty of our futures. But we kissed, and our bond strengthened.

13

Death march

January 1945

As temperatures dropped and snow started to fall in the late autumn of 1944, there were persistent rumours that the Russians were getting closer. We heard nothing official, but it was obvious that the SS were becoming worried. All of a sudden, many of the senior SS officers seemed to have disappeared. I no longer saw Kramer or Mengele or even Grese.

Initially, little changed in our day-to-day lives. Everyone was expected to work; the daily or twice-daily *Zählappell* continued, along with regular selections; and living conditions, including inadequate food and hygiene, only worsened.

After a large number of selections in October, with many sent to the gas chambers, in November this form of extermination came to a sudden end. Word came from the *Sonderkommando* that they were dismantling the gas chambers and crematoriums.

Girls who worked in the offices reported that they were being ordered to destroy documents. Some buildings were burnt to the ground.

I had little information that I could offer the other girls as reassurance. Instead, I repeated what I had been saying over and over since the start: that our best chance of survival was to stick together.

In early January, the weather now bitterly cold, we heard that we were to be marched west, into Germany and away from the approaching Russians. All the Auschwitz camps were to be 'evacuated'. Where we would go and for how long, no one knew. We couldn't be sure they wouldn't just kill us all, though I heard it said that while the Germans had no human interest in keeping us alive, they still needed prisoner labour inside the Reich to maintain their war effort. It seemed likely the SS didn't know either. We would see SS guards running here and there in what looked almost like panic. The camps seemed to be returning to the sort of chaos we had known after first arriving at Auschwitz nearly three years before. However, this disorganisation created opportunities to prepare ourselves in case there was to be a march, though once again it was impossible to help everyone. Using my connections, I organised warm clothes and boots for myself and my cousins. A group of girls broke into the kitchen and filled some bags with whatever they could find: salami, sugar, margarine and bread. Other groups of women and men did similar things to prepare themselves. Any SS who saw any of this just ignored it. By then, they were only worried about themselves.

Amongst all this commotion, Béla was able to come into my room without asking anyone's permission. We discussed whether it would be better to stay in Birkenau, if we could, and wait to be saved by the Russians. Some people had suggested hiding to avoid the marches. But there was too much uncertainty for me. What would the SS do with those who stayed, most of whom were likely to be too sick or otherwise incapable of marching? Would they shoot everyone they found, or burn them alive in their blocks? While travelling west on foot sounded dangerous, it seemed like a safer, more certain option. Béla still wasn't sure, but I told him that I would march and hoped to find him later.

———

On the morning of 18 January 1945, we were woken by guards who told us to assemble outside immediately. By then, there were only around 1000 prisoners in Camp C, though later I would learn that around 5000 women in total left Auschwitz and its sub-camps that day. In all, fifty to sixty thousand male and female prisoners from the Auschwitz camps would join what became known as the 'death marches'. Many thousands of prisoners from other concentration camps all over Europe were evacuated in their own death marches. Some moved away from the approaching Russians on the eastern front, others from the approaching British and their allies on the western front.

As we prepared to leave, SS guards handed out portions of dry bread and some thin blankets then directed us forward, in groups of around 500, out of the camp and onto a public road. We started marching in ranks of five as usual, but such order quickly disintegrated into an unstructured mess. The cold soon seeped through our clothes and then into our bones; it became immediately obvious that those of us who had had the chance to prepare ourselves with coats and proper footwear were going to outlast those who remained in their prison uniforms and open wooden clogs.

We were not alone on the roads. News of the approaching Russian army was causing long lines of German soldiers and Polish civilians to retreat west. Some were on foot, others in carts, cars or trucks that inched their way along the congested roads.

In these conditions it was impossible for me to keep track of all the girls who had been in Camp C. Instead, I turned my attention to my surviving family members: my cousins Magda Englander (who I had saved in the gypsy camp), and Piri and Irena (who were sisters); along with Ruzenka, who had been with me since the start of Birkenau and nursed me through my bout of typhus; her cousin Františka and my loyal *Rapportschreiberin* Gerda. I was like a hen with little chickens as I tried to keep our small group together.

The SS guards were nervous. They knew they would probably be shot if the Russians caught up to us, so they hurried us on. It wasn't long before some girls in the main group could no longer keep up. Weak, undernourished and unprotected from the cold, they began to stumble or fall.

And so the shooting started.

The Nazis had no patience for anyone who might slow us down. A girl who paused, bending down to straighten her clog, was shot dead. Others who fell were also shot, or left for dead in the snow. As we marched on, we came across more and more bodies left discarded on the side of the road, those from groups in front of us who had been unable to continue or not fast enough for the SS guard. But there was no time to feel any sadness. We had to concentrate on our own survival.

As the reality of our situation sank in, I urged my cousin Magda to the front of our little group. I wanted to hide her limp from the guards. The girls carrying bags of food worried they were moving too slowly, hampered by the weight. They discarded much of their load, uneaten, on the side of the road.

We were pushed on relentlessly, allowed to rest for a few minutes only occasionally. As night approached, the Nazis pointed us to nearby barns, where we lay crowded together on the straw.

———

The next morning came and, without providing any food or drink, the SS guards ordered us to get up and move.

'All on the march!' they shouted.

Those who could stand did so, but some would march no further, having died in their sleep. We stepped out into the snow and freezing cold once again.

Gerda had started the march with a bad cough, which by now had become much worse. Soon she was struggling to keep up, even with our help. A horse pulling a low wagon came by, the German at the front calling for anyone who was having trouble walking to get on. Gerda – this kind, gentle and intelligent young woman, who had worked so closely with me in Camp C – raised her hand. There was nothing I could do. We both knew her likely fate, but pretended not to. Better this than being left for dead on the road. My heart wept, as I knew I would never see her again.

Sometime later another wagon came past. I couldn't believe what I was seeing when I noticed my cousins Piri and Irena sitting at the back. How had I not noticed them falling behind?

'Irena, Piri, get off now!' I screamed. 'If I have to walk, you do too.'

I ran up to the vehicle and pulled both girls off. Irena tried to push me away, arguing that she could do what she liked. I had to slap her to make her see sense.

'What were you thinking?' I said. 'Have I not told you that the people on these carts will be shot dead as soon as they are out of sight? These Germans have no interest in saving anyone's life.'

My action almost certainly saved their lives, and both girls would go on to survive the war, though like Magda after I had slapped her in the gypsy camp, it was the slap that Irena would remember.

We came to a major road crossing where the traffic became even more chaotic, with columns of prisoners and civilians and soldiers passing each other and heading in multiple directions.

'Magda, Magda,' I heard one of the women further up the road calling back.

After a few minutes she found me.

'Magda, the men are coming from the other direction. I saw Béla, and I have asked the SS women if you could talk to him. The first guard refused but the second said okay. Come! Come!'

I followed this girl as she took me to a small clearing by the side of the intersection. And there was Béla.

An SS woman called out, 'You have five minutes.'

Béla and I realised we had no way of finding each other after the war, should we both make it home.

'I know your tattoo number,' said Béla. 'If you remember mine too, we can use them to find each other.'

'I am no good with remembering numbers,' I said.

'It's easy,' he said. 'My number is in your number.'

'How so?' I said.

'You have 2318, so 23 and 18. I have 65066. The total of my numbers is 6+5+6+6, which is 23. And my number has three sixes: 6×3 is 18. So that's 23 and 18.'

He looked very pleased with himself that he had managed to create this riddle to help me remember his number. All I could think was that we had been in the Germans' hell for so long that Béla's first instinct was that we should remember each other's numbers, not our names.

'Look for me in Michalovce,' I called to him as he walked away to rejoin his group.

————

I have few memories of the march after the first day or two. It's impossible to describe in words how our deep hunger and the deeper cold combined to diminish our last stores of energy. Hunched over, we trudged on, staying together where we could but mostly retreating into our own minds. Occasionally local villagers would throw food to us, but few dared to bend over and pick it up. It might be our last move. The further we went, the more bodies we passed: bodies of those who had been too slow, had stopped even for a moment or were too exhausted to take another step.

The guards and soldiers who marched with us seemed to have little idea where they were going, and more than once we took a wrong turn, only to be ordered to turn around and go back in the other direction. There was no opportunity to manipulate these guards in any way. At times they seemed as frightened and bewildered as us, only they had their guns to help them carve their way past anything that slowed us down too much.

After three or four days of walking, perhaps more, we came to a town – it was either Gliwice or Wodzisław Śląski (by then I was in no condition to recognise where we were). There, we were loaded onto trains, only this was not like the first transport. The wagons on this train were open, the type used to carry bulk product like coal or grain, which completely exposed us to the weather. Still, we had no food and the only water was what we could collect as melting snow. All we could do was huddle together and wait for the end of this torture.

For some, of course, the end was permanent. That any of us survived this journey is a miracle. It was perhaps another three or four days that we spent on this train, and with every passing day more girls died. I became sick myself, with difficulty breathing, but somehow stayed alive.

And then there was still more torture. We finally left the train at the Ravensbrück concentration camp in the north of Germany, where we found more disorganisation and chaos. Hardly able to walk, we were pushed towards our 'barrack', which turned out to be nothing more than a large tent sitting on bare ground. This muddy, cold earth was to be home for perhaps 3000 girls. It offered barely any more shelter from the elements than the open train carriage. I huddled with my cousins and friends in silence. I was now too ill to hold any conversation. With a heavy chest and even more difficulty breathing – perhaps it was pneumonia, perhaps hypothermia, I never knew – I allowed myself to consider that this, perhaps, was finally going to be my end.

However, fate had other plans.

A group of prisoners started to bring us soup and tea. Just as I realised some of them were speaking French, I heard one of them call, *'Magda est là! Magda est là!'* 'Magda is here! Magda is here!'

They were some of the same French women for whom, back in Birkenau, I had been *Blockälteste* for the first time. I tried to look pleased to see them, but could hardly see by then, let alone smile. They told me they had been looking out for me since they first heard that women were being transferred from Birkenau.

'Magda, we will look after you,' they said.

They carried me to their block. Because these women were mostly non-Jewish political prisoners with intellectual back-grounds, they had been given work in the offices and were living in better conditions. They were able to help me shower, feed me well and provide medicine. They gave me a bed to sleep on. I was returned to the tent with my cousins and friends only for one thing: the roll calls. They told me I needed to get better because in just a few days my group was likely to be moved on to another camp, and that this would involve another march.

As I started to recover, these women told me about their life in Ravensbrück since they had been transferred here two years earlier. This was a camp that housed almost entirely women. Through-out 1943 it had not been very crowded, populated mainly with political prisoners and only a few Jews and Roma. As such, Ravens-brück was not an extermination camp, as Auschwitz was, but a working camp. There was more attention given to putting the inmates to work in factories than sending them to gas chambers. In fact, Ravensbrück had no gas chamber; if women needed to be 'removed', they were sent to other camps for that purpose. The French women worried, however, that this was changing. There were rumours that a gas chamber was being built. In the last six months, the population had grown rapidly and the SS emphasis had shifted towards killing rather than work.

After a few days, thanks to these wonderful women, I was feeling a little better. At least I was strong enough to walk again.

On one of our last days in Ravensbrück, a strange thing happened when, all of a sudden, SS officer Johann Schwarzhuber appeared in front of me. He was the *Schutzhaftlagerführer* of the men's camp at Auschwitz who had agreed with me that we Slovakians needed new dresses in Birkenau in 1943. Now he was in charge of the women's camp at Ravensbrück, so was ultimately responsible for the atrocious conditions we found ourselves in. He was dressed more elegantly than usual, in full uniform, cap and highly polished boots.

He said to me, 'I've been looking for you.'

He showed me two identity documents, one with my name on it, and told me he had a plane waiting to fly him to Switzerland, and that he wanted me to go with him.

'I am well established and will look after you well,' he said.

I couldn't think. I didn't know what to say. Why would I want to follow this man?

Eventually I said, 'I have all my surviving family here and I cannot leave them. Sorry, but they need me.'

He urged me some more but I continued to refuse. I was saved by the call to assemble for *Zählappell*.

14

Malchow

February 1945

Ravensbrück was grossly overcrowded and chaotic, which is probably why the SS decided to move some of us to its surrounding sub-camps. They performed another selection – by this point I don't know how they found anyone who was fit for work – and sent us back onto the road on foot. Once again my group and I were struggling through snow, once again we were frozen to the marrow within only a few hours. Once again the SS were brutal to those who fell behind or simply couldn't go on.

By the end of perhaps the second day, there was nothing left of any 'rest' we'd had at Ravensbrück, which for most had been no more than a few days of filth and starvation. We reached a huge deserted storehouse in a small forest and were ordered inside. There was no food and the only water was what we could gather as snow. There were no toilets either. Everyone collapsed, wondering how we could possibly find the strength to continue.

With my strength depleted to almost nothing once more, I started to fade in and out of consciousness.

All of a sudden, my mother stood before me. She reminded me of the blessing of the Belzer rabbi and the mission he had seen for me. She told me there were still more lives to be saved. I had to go on. Then she held a large bowl of warm, round scones in front of me. When I reached out, she pulled the bowl away.

'Can't you see I'm so hungry?' I said. 'Why won't you let me have any?'

She said, 'First you have to promise me something.'

'What is that?' I said.

'That if you marry after the war and have children, you will bring them up to be Jewish,' she said.

'I am hardly alive!' I said. 'When will I be free, when would I be able to marry and have children?'

'You just promise me,' she said.

'I promise,' I said.

At that moment someone touched my arm. Startled, I opened my eyes and saw a woman in front of me holding a huge bowl of potatoes, the steam rising from them. When I looked around there were a number of other women also with these bowls.

I was in no condition to question how these women had come in past the SS guards. Perhaps they had bribed them. Perhaps the guards had left us. And where had the women come from? They must have been sympathetic locals. In any case, they had food – good, hot food – for us. They were angels sent to save us and no one really cared how or why they were there.

We may have stayed for two nights in that storehouse – by then, time meant nothing – before the SS came inside and shouted, *'Raus, raus!'* 'Out, out!'

We stumbled out onto the crowded road once again.

Our group became mixed up with a group of German soldiers who were marching in the same direction. These were members of the *Wehrmacht*, the German armed forces that were separate, at least officially, from the Nazi-controlled SS. Two of these *Wehrmacht*, who were a bit older, spoke to me. They revealed that our destination was the Malchow camp, a sub-camp of Ravensbrück that had been established to provide labour to an ammunition plant.

'What is your profession?' one asked me.

'I am a kindergarten teacher,' I said. 'I know nothing about ammunition.'

'Ah, but you are exactly who we need,' he said. 'I know the *Lagerführerin* and I know there is a group of around forty young girls in Malchow, about sixteen years of age, who arrived there only yesterday. I will make sure you will be their *Blockälteste*.'

I wondered if these were some of the 800 we had saved in Camp C.

It's surreal to think about, but this conversation, which took place as we continued to drag our weakened bodies along snow-covered roads, gave me a little energy. The idea of being back in a camp, and having some routine again, spurred me on. Was this what I had been reduced to . . . the idea that a concentration camp would be some form of relief?

———

Somehow, after all we had been through since leaving Auschwitz, I still had my 'chickens' with me when we arrived at Malchow: Ruzenka and Františka, Irena and Piri, and Magda Englander. Gerda . . . poor Gerda. She was the only one lost to us.

The German soldier kept his word and he took me and our group straight to the woman in charge of the younger girls, who were indeed some of those Gerda and I had saved from Mengele. I was so happy to know they were still alive.

Surprisingly, the accommodation was not as bad as we had expected. We had beds with mattresses – thin, but still mattresses – and we had better food than we were used to. It was still dreadful – this was not a hotel – but even a bed with no mattress is more comfortable than lying on the cold, bare ground. The food improved further after Františka volunteered to help in the stores. She was well practiced at organising and would return most nights with some salami or bread or other treat to be shared. In all of this we were fortunate. Malchow was only a small camp – there were just ten or twelve barracks and, at this time, only a hundred or so inmates in each. Somehow it was more relaxed than Birkenau, with the improved conditions and without the incessant beatings. This helped us to recover some of the strength we had lost during the death march.

We had no idea how long we were going to be there, or where we might go next, but at least we were not living with constant fear.

And then, about two weeks after we had arrived, everything changed.

First, production at the munitions factory slowed to almost nothing, so there were fewer workers required. This was apparently due to those running the plant no longer having access to the raw materials they needed for their work. Then, over just two days, thousands more women arrived after their own marches from Auschwitz and other camps close to both the eastern and western fronts. Like Ravensbrück, Malchow now became severely over-crowded as the Nazis evacuated more and more prisoners away from the front lines in the hope of preserving their free source of labour. In most blocks, there were now around 500 in a space big enough for just 100.

As all this was going on I came across Leah, the Czech Jewish girl who had been a runner when I was *Blockälteste* of the *Stabsgebäude*, the elite block. She told me she had been trans-ferred to Malchow for doing something wrong – I didn't ask what, but remember thinking it seemed a strange punishment to be sent to a better camp. Anyway, she had always been clever and capable, and by then had worked her way into a position as an advisor to the *Lagerkommandant* of the camp.

'Magda, we need you,' she said. 'You have experience with large numbers of people, and there is so much typhus and other disease in all these newcomers. They are crowded so close together. We will find someone else to look after the other girls.'

I had no say in this, but soon found myself as *Blockälteste* of 1000 women in a single, open barn-like building separate from the main accommodation blocks. They called it the canteen. Another girl, Eta, was the *Blockälteste* for another thousand.

Conditions deteriorated and were soon worse than anything I had encountered in the last three years. No animal should be kept in such conditions, let alone humans. This enormous building had nothing but straw on the floor and little protection from the cold. The women were already so weak after the ordeal of the march, most without any coats or shoes, that it was a miracle they had made it that far. Now they had to survive this. The camp was simply unprepared for the number of new arrivals. Food was scarce. I did what I could to share it evenly, stirring the soup to bring the thicker part to the top, but there was never nearly enough. It was all filth and starvation, the torture of constant cold, and death. Having made it this far, so many could go on no longer, and passed away where they lay.

There was no work either – not for most, anyway. A few continued to work in the munitions factory and a few outside the camp – I never knew exactly what they did. A small number, such as myself, worked as functionaries. This left most lying or sitting on the ground, slowly starving to death. Typhus soon started to spread, and while my helpers and I tried to keep the ill separate from others, there was little I could do to prevent the disease from taking hold.

———

The days and weeks wore on like this, and became even worse when *SS-Aufseherin* Luise Danz arrived at Malchow. This was the same cruel SS officer who had taken over from Grese and forced me out as *Lagerälteste* of Camp C for a few days. As soon as Danz arrived, the violence and depravity in Malchow increased. She was given the role of *Oberaufseherin*, head of the female guards, and restricted the limited food to those capable of work, leaving others to starve to death. She immediately encouraged the guards to use more beatings, while she roamed the camp, whipping anyone for any reason.

What could I do to stop her? There had to be something. Finally she gave me the opportunity herself.

'Hellinger,' she called to me one morning. 'I want you to be *Arbeitdienst*. You will start immediately.'

The role of 'work organiser' involved dividing people up to go to work: who would go to an outside *Kommando*, who to the factory and so on. Many of those in functionary roles wanted this job because it was more administrative, so a little easier.

'Why would you choose me?' I asked.

'Because I have respect for you,' she said.

'You do? Why?'

'You remember when I pushed you out as *Lagerälteste*? You didn't for one moment question this decision or beg me to leave you in the role. You weren't afraid. You didn't need the glory of being the *Lagerälteste*. You didn't try to bribe me. You just accepted it without complaint. That made an impression on me, and for that you have my respect.'

I didn't understand how Danz's mind worked, but I told myself that if this terrible woman wanted me to do this job, and if she really had some respect for me, I would do as she wished without objection. Being in this role and closer to Danz might create opportunities for me to influence her behaviour, at least a little, in the same way I had tempered Grese's enthusiasm for her whip.

While talking to Edith, one of the girls I had cracked lice with back in the early days of Birkenau, I remembered that she was talented at sketching portraits with charcoal. Perhaps I could win Danz over a little by appealing to her vanity?

A few days later I told Danz about Edith. 'Would you like a portrait of yourself? You just have to sit for her. I'm sure you will like it.'

She agreed with enthusiasm, so I organised the materials needed and sent Edith to Danz with an instruction to work slowly.

'The longer Danz is sitting, the longer she will not be hitting anyone,' I said.

Edith was very clever. She talked to Danz and took her time and even stopped and asked Danz to return for another sitting. She did this two or three times. Finally, the picture was done and Danz was very happy with it.

It was so strange, but for a few minutes here or there, Danz started to talk to me about herself, almost like Grese had done. This was different though, because Danz was closer to my age than Grese. I think she imagined me a friend, rather than a sister as Grese had seemed to, though I never gave back any more than was needed to encourage her to talk. She admitted to me that the SS intended for every prisoner in Malchow to die eventually, and this was why they weren't providing enough food. Once, seeming to forget who she was talking to, she boasted about her ability to beat women to death at the roll calls.

All this talk was her weakness, and it was to be exploited.

'I have a brother who is fighting on the Russian front,' she told me one day. 'I am so worried about him.'

This gave me another idea.

I asked around the camp for someone who could read palms and soon found a gypsy amongst the Hungarian women. I told her about Danz and her brother and shared my plan with her.

'*Oberaufseherin*,' I said the next morning. 'I know you are worried about the future, with the Russians approaching. I have someone who can read palms. Would you like your fortune told?'

Of course, she agreed. I took the palm reader to her room and left her there.

The woman held Danz's palm and inspected it carefully, making various comments about how she would have a long life, that she would live out her days in her beloved Germany and so on.

After a time, the palm reader said, 'I see someone worrying about you, a long way away. It is a man . . . a soldier.'

Danz's eyes grew wide.

'My brother!' she cried. 'It must be him. He is fighting in Russia.'

The fortune teller frowned.

'This person is worried for you, though.'

Now Danz frowned too.

'Worried? Why?'

The woman continued to look deeply into Danz's palm.

'He's thinking that the war is about to end, and he's afraid that you will be punished. He's really worried with all his heart.'

'I don't know what you mean,' said Danz. 'How do you know this?'

'It's written clearly in your palm. He – your brother, you say – is very worried. He is really thinking about you with all his heart and he loves you so much. But he's scared for you that you will have a bad ending for beating the inmates.'

Afterwards, Danz came running to find me.

'Magda, this woman is wonderful. Do you know what she told me?' She shared the whole conversation with me, and finally said, 'Do you think I should stop hitting people with the whip?'

I said, 'I don't know. But if that is your brother's wish—'

'It seems to be.'

From then on, Danz stopped being so cruel, and stopped using the whip – at least enough that I no longer saw it happening. It was unbelievable that a fortune teller was all it took to stop this violent woman in her tracks, at least for a while.

15

Liberation

I didn't realise it at the time, but Danz was the last of the Nazis to know my name.

As what remained of the winter's snow melted away, the sight and sounds of warplanes in the skies above us became more and more persistent. When they were low enough, we could make out some as German and others as British, or occasionally Russian. We were hearing more and more news of the approaching Russians, and with that the Germans became more panicked. Soon, just as had happened at Auschwitz, many of the senior SS disappeared.

In early April a large group of women had been selected and marched towards the nearby railway tracks. We first heard that they were to be transported to another camp, though Danz told me she expected the train would be bombed by Allied aircraft along the route. History suggests she was wrong and the women eventually arrived at another camp, though I don't know what happened to them after that.

Fewer prisoners in the camp did not mean improved conditions. If anything, the situation worsened as the SS who remained were now interested only in their own survival. Food was available only every second or third day, and never enough. There was little I could do but try to make sure everyone got something, and also to try to maintain a little order. At least I no longer needed to stop Danz and others beating the inmates.

Finally – I didn't know the date, but apparently it was 1 May 1945 – those of us still at Malchow, still alive and still able to walk, were rounded up by the remaining SS and ordered to march out of the camp. Where we were going I don't think anyone knew – it was just west, further into Germany and away from the advancing Russians.

Now there seemed to be even more civilian traffic than there had been on the first march: carts laden with baskets and furniture, children and even animals. In the confusion though, there were also groups coming the other way, perhaps responding to rumours that the Allied forces were approaching from the opposite direction. It was a mishmash. No one knew what was happening.

Perhaps it was the warmer weather, or just the fact that there were now very few SS guards, but this march did not feel as threatening as the earlier ones. It was simply chaotic. As before, I did what I could to keep my small band of family together as groups of prisoners from other camps and other groups of civilians blended into one long tangle of humanity.

About a day after we started, I heard voices calling my name.

'Magda, Magda.'

They sounded familiar, but their accents were out of place. I turned to see three of the women from the Russian village who I had been responsible for in Birkenau nearly eighteen months earlier. They were some of the young women who, after the boys had been removed, had been transported away to work as nurses in German hospitals. By a miracle we had now crossed paths again.

We kissed and hugged each other as old friends, the Russian women explaining that they had left the hospitals and were now acting as partisans for the approaching forces.

'We are so glad we found you,' one of them said. 'The Russian soldiers are very close and will liberate all the camp prisoners. But we were thinking about you. If someone points a finger at you and says you were in a position of authority, some of the Russian soldiers will see you as an enemy. Some of them are seeking revenge and they will most likely rape you, possibly kill you.

'You need to come with us. We will hide you until we can explain who you are and the wonderful things you did for us Russians at Birkenau.'

The concern on these girls' faces was genuine. It seemed I had to trust them and take them seriously.

'What about my girls?' I said, pointing at my hens. 'I don't want to leave them.'

'They will be okay. The only people under threat are those prisoners who, like you, worked closely with the Germans as functionaries, as *Blockältesten* and *Lagerältesten* and so on. We know you were forced into these positions, but some of our soldiers don't understand this and think you were collaborating.'

In the end I negotiated that they should take three of us, because Ruzenka and Františka had also been in positions of responsibility.

'We are living in a flour mill nearby,' one of the Russian girls explained. 'It will be a base when the army arrives, so we will hide you in the woods until we can get agreement from the soldiers that they won't hurt you. Then we will bring you to the mill as well.'

And so, after checking that there were no SS around, we wished good luck to the other girls of our group and the Russian women led the three of us into the woods. After a short time they built us a small hut of branches and leaves, gave us some food and told us we must stay in hiding until they came to get us. They told us it might be a few days until they were back.

The weather was dry and not cold, and the forest floor was soft, so we mostly slept while we waited. We were deep enough into the woods that we couldn't hear any noise from the road. We could hear aircraft overhead, though, and, in the distance, the sounds of what might have been gunfire or explosions.

Eventually, after three nights, the Russian women returned.

'Come with us,' they said. 'The men want to see you. They want to thank you for what you did. Don't worry, they will not harm you.'

We followed these women back to the mill, and were greeted by a group of around forty Russians, male soldiers and other women who had been operating as partisans. The building had been set up as a temporary barrack, with stretcher beds and a dining hall. We were welcomed generously, and when it came time to eat, they sat us down at the head table as their guests of honour, then brought more food and drink than we had seen in years. It was all quite surreal, and my basic Russian was not enough to know what was being said most of the time, but it was nice to feel welcome. After the meal ended, I stood up and started to collect some of the plates, but a voice called out, '*Nyet!* You are our guests. Let others do the work.'

We rested in this place for a couple of days until the soldiers announced that they had to move on. They loaded up their trucks and said goodbye, pointing us back to the main road where we could continue on our way.

As we rejoined the throngs on the road, the atmosphere had changed. There were no German soldiers or SS anywhere. News reached us that Hitler was dead and German surrender was imminent. As the cloud that had enveloped Europe for six years finally began to lift, there was a sense of relief that soon broke into celebration, even amongst many local German people. The racket, the singing, the dancing. Hitler was gone and with him his authoritarian rule. The Nazis had surrendered in Europe.

The war was over.

———

For Ruzenka, Františka and me, along with millions of others across Europe, there was little chance to acknowledge the reality that we had somehow survived the war. We were alive, and no longer needed to live in fear. But we were also in the north of Germany, a sort of no-man's land now, and hundreds of kilometres from home.

As thousands moved along the roads, information was shared via word of mouth. Someone would say they'd heard there was a meeting place for Poles in one town, or for French in another. We eventually came across a Czech man who told us of a place where Czechs and Hungarians were gathering, and that there were trucks that might transport us to our home towns, or at least closer to them. We took his advice and headed south, in the direction he pointed us.

After the initial celebrations, we witnessed a lot of unpleasant behaviour as we continued to walk. There was still so much anger, especially amongst those who had been imprisoned by the Nazis, and unfortunately some of this anger was directed at ordinary German people. Others, including some of the victorious soldiers, took advantage of the chaotic situation. Homes were broken into and shops were looted, by both armed soldiers and former inmates.

Finally, we reached a rough camp that had been established by the Russians. I don't remember where it was, but here we found several hundred people. There were many Hungarians and Czechoslovakians, and here and there we recognised other survivors from Birkenau. Amongst these I found Mrs Mordkovic, a friend of my mother's who Dr Gisella Perl had been able to save. We stayed together with others who we knew. There was not yet much organisation, just groups of Russian soldiers and a few officials who didn't seem to know much about what was going on. Somehow, there was food – perhaps from the Red Cross or a similar organisation, though my memories of this time are as muddled as the place itself.

I guess it was a natural thing, but some women who recognised me from Birkenau started to turn to me as a leader again, as if I was still *Lagerälteste*.

'Magda, I need your help.'

'Magda, where can I find . . .?'

Magda. Magda. Magda.

'Leave me alone!' I exclaimed to one woman. 'I am no longer your leader.'

I used a line from a Hungarian song: *'Söpörtem eleget, söpörjön már más'*, which roughly translates as, 'I have swept enough. Let someone else sweep now.'

But they kept coming anyway.

A group of Hungarian girls approached me.

'Magda, please help us. The Russians want to send some of us away to help them with harvesting or to work in their factories. They are saying that because Hungary was in alliance with Germany, we are the enemy. But we just want to go home. We know you speak some Russian – please will you speak to the commander?'

I went to the commander. 'These girls are not your enemies. They are Jewish – that is why the Hungarians threw them out. They are not friends of the Hungarian government any more than they are friends of the Nazis. They have lived in concentration camps for months, some for years. They have a right to return to their homes and find any family they have left.'

The commander stared at me with tired eyes.

'Da, da,' he said. 'Yes, yes.' And that was the end of that.

Finally some trucks started to arrive that could carry people back to their home countries, or at least closer. Groups were identified and offered transport. We waited our turn, but it didn't seem to come, and eventually Mrs Mordkovic came to me.

'Magda, there is one last thing you have to do. They won't take us. There are trucks heading to Prague, but they are only

229

taking the Czechs, not the Slovaks. They will leave us here to rot. Please Magda, you have influence. Please speak to the committee.' She was referring to the committee that was managing the transport.

'Okay,' I said. 'I'll see what I can do.'

I went to find the head of the committee, who explained that there weren't enough trucks to transport everyone. They would get to us eventually.

'It's not enough,' I said. 'There are very few of us. There are just 300 of us left. We only need two or three trucks. Do you understand what the Slovakian Jews have been through? Despite being good citizens, we were the first transported – our own government paid the Germans to take us away. That was over three years ago, and those of us who remain have survived the camps for all that time. Many of these girls have spent every day since wondering whether any of their family members are still alive.

'I know there are trucks. I heard President Beneš has just returned from exile and is in Slovakia. If I was his cousin, there would be a truck for me.'

The man looked at me with a strange smile.

'As a matter of fact, I am a cousin of President Beneš,' he said.

Hearing that, I banged the table with my fist and said, 'Well, for you there would be a truck!'

'I guess you are right,' he said. He looked through the papers in front of him and then back at me. 'There will be trucks this evening that will take the Slovakians as far as Prague. From there you will have to work out other arrangements to take you to your home towns.'

I thanked him and ran back to tell Mrs Mordkovic.

'I knew only you could do it!' she cried as she hugged me tight.

———

Ruzenka, Františka and I arrived in Prague and found ourselves in a large hall crowded with hundreds of people who had found their way back from all over Europe. There was so much noise and hustle and bustle as we tried to make our way to one of the counters where officials were registering new arrivals.

When we finally made it to the front, we were each given 500 Czech koruna to assist with transport and issued with identification in the form of a small registration booklet containing our name and the destination we ultimately hoped to reach.

In my booklet I wrote Palestine. I had no intention of staying in the country that had thrown me out like dirty linen. In my mind I would return to Michalovce to find out if any of my family had survived, and I would then emigrate to Palestine and start a new life.

As we started to make enquiries about how we might find our way to our homes, which were still over 700 kilometres away, Ruzenka learnt that her village had been almost totally destroyed by bombings, so I convinced her to come home with me. Františka would travel with us to a certain point and then find her own way home near the end.

Amongst all the people in the hall, there was a buzz of constant questioning. Everyone was looking for someone, and everyone had heard a rumour that such-and-such had last been seen on the road in some small town, or at a refugee camp, or at a concentration camp. Or that they had not been seen for months. Cries of agony and ecstasy burst into the air as bad and good news was shared.

'Magda! Magda!'

I looked over and recognised one of the inmate doctors from Birkenau calling to me over the heads of the crowd.

'Béla,' he yelled. 'Béla is alive! Béla is alive!'

He pushed his way through the crowd until he could speak to me properly.

'You should go to him,' he said. 'He left for Michalovce a few days ago in the hope of finding you there. He has been looking and looking for you.'

I thanked the man and said I would try to find Béla.

The truth was, Béla had not been at the front of my mind. I had thought about him, but I had not counted on finding him again. Perhaps I didn't want to get too hopeful after all we had been through. Until that moment, I hadn't even known if he had survived the rest of the death march and the subsequent months. Still, the first thing to do now was to get back to Michalovce. If Béla was there, that would be good. We could talk and discuss each other's plans from there. Perhaps he would join me in Palestine.

There was no way to easily return to Michalovce. None of the trains were working as normal, and most that did operate were running a limited service due to damaged sections of the tracks. It was the same on the roads, with long sections pot-holed by bombing. We decided we would just keep moving, walking when there was no other way, and over a number of days Ruzenka and I were finally back where it had all started.

Of course, my town was a very different place. I found most of it still intact – it seemed to have been spared the worst of the fighting – but it was immediately clear that this was not the town I had left.

Finally we arrived at my house, which I was relieved to find had not been 'acquired' – it had become a common practice for empty Jewish properties to be commandeered by non-Jews, who saw this as their right. Inside, I discovered my brother Ernest was already there. We hugged as he confirmed what I had already heard from others: that our parents and youngest brother had been murdered after being transported to Łuków only a month or so after I had been deported.

Ernest took us inside, where he had a number of friends and relatives with him. The house was bare. While it had not been taken from us, the furniture had all been stolen, presumably by people who thought we would have no further use for it. After all the others had gone, Ernest and our cousin Béla Hellinger constructed some makeshift beds with straw-filled sacks for mattresses.

I asked Ernest if Béla Blau had called at the house, but he had not seen him. I decided I would ask around the next day.

That night Ruzenka and I rested in freedom for the first time in many years, though I don't recall really allowing myself to believe it at the time. There was still so much uncertainty about the future. While I had made it back home, it did not feel like home. Perhaps only then was the loss of my parents starting to sink in.

———

The first person I visited the next day was my best friend Marta, along with her husband Bandi and beautiful baby girl Eva. Spending this time with Marta transported me back to happier times more than anything else in Michalovce. It soon felt like yesterday. She gave me pillows, sheets and blankets for our beds, and invited Ruzenka and me for a delicious dinner.

Marta never asked about the camp, and I didn't tell.

I think she intuitively knew that I only wanted to look forward, so that's what we talked about. She told me of their plans to move to Argentina with her whole family.

And there was something she wanted me to tell her about: Béla.

It seemed that when Béla had been in town looking for me about two weeks earlier, someone had directed him to talk to Marta. He told her he needed to return to Žilina, but left a letter for her to pass on to me. In that letter, he asked me to go to Žilina, giving me the address of his sister, Aranka Platzner. He had told his sister that he wanted to marry me.

'But I hardly know him,' I told Ruzenka.

'You didn't have the chance to get to know him in the camp,' she replied, and of course she was right. 'Anyway, he made all that effort to come here and find you. He must be serious about you.'

With each day, there was news of others who had made it home. I learnt that Irena, Piri and Magda Englander, who we had left after Malchow, had all made it back. Every time someone arrived back in our community, there was another small celebration, joy in our hearts at finding each other alive despite having lost so many. Everyone shared whatever food and other provisions they had. No one talked of what we had been through, instead turning their attention to recovery and the rebuilding of lives.

Finally though, with nothing else to do straightaway, I decided that I would travel the 350 kilometres to Žilina, but only after a few days of rest. Ruzenka, who was a good dressmaker, made me a beautiful blue silk dress to travel in. Sensing my continuing hesitation, she took me to the station and made sure that I got on the train.

———

I soon found myself knocking on Béla's sister's door.

'Hello, I am Magda,' I said.

'Magda! I am Aranka, Béla's sister. It is so lovely to meet you.' She asked me inside, and then told me that her husband, Jancsi, and Béla had gone to Prague for a few days to sort out some business.

'Béla insisted that if you came you must stay and wait for him. He will be back in only a day or so.'

Aranka couldn't have made me feel more welcome, though it felt strange staying with people who were, despite the loose connection, strangers to me. Nevertheless, I couldn't have gone anywhere even if I wanted to. Aranka's ten-year-old son Tommy made sure of that. Perhaps sensing my discomfort, he took me under his wing and chaperoned me everywhere I went. I went swimming, for long walks and even met some old friends to go to the cinema. Tommy was with me all the time.

One day, Tommy turned to me with a very serious face. 'Please don't run away from here. You know, Magda, my uncle loves you very much. He will be very unhappy if you go. And by the way, he is the best man in the world.'

At that I had to laugh.

The next day, Aranka took me shopping and to visit some friends. She introduced me as her sister-in-law . . . which was a little hard to deny in the moment.

Béla and Jancsi arrived home that evening. When he saw me, Béla lifted me up and danced around the room, his blue eyes shining.

Not long afterwards, he placed a ring on my finger. I hadn't admitted to myself that I was ready for this, but deep down I knew that saying 'yes' to Béla was the right decision.

The war was over, and we had somehow survived. It was time to move on.

PART TWO

MY MOTHER MOVES ON

16

How to build a new life

It is obviously impossible to truly comprehend the camp life my mother described in her story. The conditions, the cruelty, the killing. Words only go so far. And then to return home to confirm that your parents and most of your family have perished, along with countless other family, friends and acquaintances . . .

I have in my possession a copy of the Hellingers' family tree, the extended family of my grandfather, Ignac Hellinger. On that list, someone has highlighted all those who perished during the Holocaust. There are 117 highlighted names – 117 deaths from just one family line. Of over 4000 Jews in Michalovce in 1940, only around 600 survived the war. Fewer than 300 of over 7000 women and girls deported to Auschwitz from Slovakia survived. Across Slovakia, over 80 per cent of the pre-war Jewish population was murdered.

But to those of us who try to comprehend these numbers, they are, in the end, still just numbers.

To Magda, Béla and others who returned to their home towns, they were people. Parents and siblings, husbands and wives. Children. Teachers, shopkeepers, colleagues. People you passed on the street each day. In short, the people who provided the structure around which your life was built. All gone.

How can you move forward after all that?

The answer, as my mother always told me, was that you simply have no choice. What else are you going to do? Just as people like Magda and Béla adapted to 'life' in the camps, they adapted again to life after the camps.

———

Magda Hellinger officially married Béla Blau in Prague on 13 March 1946, though they started their new lives together well before that. Dates and formalities were nebulous concepts in the early months after the war.

With no money other than a small amount of government assistance, Magda and Béla travelled to Prague, where Béla set about trying to find some work. Thanks to a Czech government program, an opportunity arose for Holocaust survivors to take over abandoned businesses and factories in the region of Sudety, or Sudentenland in German. This was the predominantly German-speaking region Hitler had annexed before the outbreak of the war, and which was now, once again, Czechoslovakian territory. Soon after the war, most of the German population of the region was expelled into Germany, leaving many businesses empty. As soon as this program was announced, Béla went away to explore the options and choose a business for him and Magda to operate together.

Magda and Béla moved to a small town, Jiříkov, 130 kilometres north of Prague and right on the new border with
Germany. There, Magda discovered her husband had chosen a
fabric shop and haberdashery, in keeping with his previous experience as a textile salesman. It was a tiny store, with small living
quarters above, accessed by a narrow spiral staircase. The store
had very little stock and, worse still, it was at the very end of the
main street.

'You chose this place for us to build a livelihood?' Magda said.

Béla looked a little down. 'I can't stand the idea of being
around a lot of people.'

Magda wished she had travelled with Béla to help him choose;
she was sure she would have found something a little more viable.
But she was also starting to understand the damage that the war
had done to her new husband.

Béla had lost his first wife and his son, been forced to work
in outside *Kommandos*, including in the brutal *Strafkommando*,
punishment brigade, and survived particularly sadistic *Zählappelle*.
Then he had his own tortuous experiences in the last months of
the war.

As Birkenau was about to be evacuated, Béla and the men he
was with were removed back to Auschwitz main camp. Despite
rumours that the camp was likely to be bombed 'to make it
disappear', he decided to hide until the Germans had gone. He
hid under a bed and fell asleep, and woke in the middle of the
night to absolute silence. Had the Germans left already? He went
outside and found two of his friends who had worked with him
in Kanada, and they convinced him to walk with them. That
was when he joined the march, a day or so before he and Magda
would find each other at the crossroads.

After he and Magda went their separate ways on the march, the group Béla was with trudged on until they eventually arrived at the Mauthausen camp in Austria. Many died or were killed along the way. When they reached the camp, they were stripped of what clothes they had and given much worse rags.

Béla had lost much more than just his better uniform, for quite a strange reason that had its origins with Magda back in Birkenau.

While Magda was *Lagerälteste* of Camp C, an older woman from Bratislava had come to her and said, 'I am a rich woman, with money in banks in England and many other places. I am much older than you and I don't think I am going to survive the war, but you probably will. I see the work you are doing here and how you are helping so many. To show my gratitude, I am giving you a cheque for one thousand pounds that you can cash after the war.'

This wasn't a proper cheque – the woman couldn't have kept a cheque book in Auschwitz – but instead she had written a note with the necessary details on a fragile piece of paper. Magda thanked her for the 'cheque', put it away carefully and didn't give it another thought until she was about to leave Birkenau at the end. She hid it in her coat until she and Béla met at the crossroads where, for some reason, she thought perhaps it would be safer with him. Béla hid the note in a hem of his uniform, but there was no way he could remove it or hide it when the uniform was taken from him at Mauthausen. Who knows if they would ever have been able to cash it, but they never had the chance to try. The money would have been very helpful.

After about a month in appalling conditions and with little food, Béla and some others were sent to a Mauthausen subcamp,

Gusen II, where labour was needed to repair the fuel tanks and wings of damaged Messerschmitt aircraft. This was a little easier, as there was not much work to do. By that time the Germans couldn't access supplies, and there weren't enough parts to do the work required. Nevertheless, it was still a concentration camp, with scarce food, frequent beatings and constant fear. In early May they were moved to another subcamp under construction near the town of Gunskirchen. On the way there, a Wehrmachts soldier, an older man, told Béla these new camps were the secret to how Hitler was going to win the war after all. The soldier was very wrong. Less than a week later, the war was over and the American army liberated the camp.

This was as much as Béla ever told Magda or any of us about his time after Auschwitz. He never wanted to talk about it much, and I suspect he experienced and witnessed some terrible things. Either way, for a long time he had great difficulty moving ahead, and the scars remained with him for the rest of his life.

———

Their new home and store were not ideal, but they had to make do. Magda and Béla travelled around looking for merchandise. In Prague, Magda found a large quantity of silk that she was able to purchase on consignment, and this ended up being the star attraction for the little business. There was little silk in the region, so people came from more and more distant places to buy from them. Slowly, slowly, they started to build up their business.

Soon after Magda became pregnant with me, her first child, word arrived that Ruzenka had married Magda's cousin

Béla Hellinger, who she had met on their very first night back in Michalovce. Magda and Béla were invited to visit, so the shop was temporarily closed and they travelled the 800 kilometres back to Michalovce. Magda remembered this as a lovely reunion with the happy couple and with other surviving relatives she had not seen since Birkenau. Another cousin was there, Jolan, who Magda had been able to help in the camp, as were uncle Moishe Mendel and his son. Despite his age and how poorly he was when he arrived at Birkenau, Moishe had managed to survive.

Sadly, this was likely the last time that Magda saw Ruzenka. The next year she tragically lost her life during childbirth. We could never be sure whether Ruzenka's health had been compromised by her time in the camps, though it has since been clearly established that the starvation and deprivation of the concentration camps and ghettoes had long-lasting health effects on many survivors, and often on their children as well.

I was born on 5 July 1946 and named Vera Maya. I was apparently a very contented child, which was a good thing because Magda still needed to run the shop while Béla travelled to find new supplies. She would attend to me upstairs and then, when the bell rang to signal that someone had come into the shop, she would set me safely aside and run down the spiral stairs to serve the customer. Magda must have gone up and down that tiny spiral staircase thousands of times. Sometimes she would feed me, wrap me up tightly and let me sleep in my pram in the small backyard while she attended to customers. Apparently I loved being outside, no matter how cold it was, and didn't mind at all when flurries of snow built up on top of me because my mother was too busy in the store to pull me inside. I became so used to the cold air that I would cry in my cot unless the bedroom window was left open for snow to drift inside. I guess that explains why I've always loved the snow.

Eighteen months after I was born, my sister Eva arrived on 12 December 1947, and for a while our parents lived a good, peaceful and free life. They worked hard and enjoyed a strong community.

Food was scarce, with rationing still in place. Later, my mother often repeated one sad but also humorous story of this time. As our shop was on the main street, Mum was able to put Eva in her cot and sit me in the upstairs front window of our apartment. She would tell me not to move, then visit nearby stores to do her grocery shopping. As she moved between stores, she would look up and wave to me in the window, keeping an eye on me. One day, she returned home to hear Eva crying loudly as she came in the door, so she dropped her bags and ran up the spiral staircase to see what was wrong. She returned downstairs a little while later to see the Great Dane from next door scoffing the last of a month's supply of meat rations from the shopping bags in the doorway!

As she had promised her mother in her dream on the death march, Mum brought Eva and me up as Jews. She also taught us to be kind, generous and sharing in the same way her mother had taught her. This backfired one afternoon when some local families visited. I must have been about three – I only know about this from my mother's retelling – but I managed to find a box of chocolates, which were a rare commodity due to the rationing. Without asking, I proceeded to hand the chocolates around to my young friends. When Mum discovered this, she was torn: the chocolates were quite precious, but I'd only been doing what she'd taught me.

As my parents' small business started to thrive, there were signs that their newfound freedom might be short-lived. The Communist Party won elections in the Czech regions in 1946, and then in 1948 President Beneš ceded power to the communists, fearing the Soviets would take over anyway. For people like Magda and Béla, this meant a new form of totalitarianism started to impinge on their lives.

First it was small things. A lady came into the shop one time and chose some expensive silk. She asked to pay a little later, and as Béla was always good-hearted, he allowed her to do so. However, she continued to avoid paying until eventually Béla had to insist. At this, the woman told him her husband worked for the tax inspectorate. A few days later an inspector came and checked the business's books and imposed a large fine for some entirely fabricated tax error.

Then Béla was pressured to join the Communist Party. Doing so would have provided him with some protection, but he didn't want to join. Sure enough, before long the business was confiscated and we were forced to start all over again.

Had Magda and Béla survived the worst oppression imaginable at the hands of the Nazis, only to find themselves beholden to new masters in the form of the Communist Party?

Finally, Magda had had enough. With Israel's independence, she decided it was time to fulfil her desire to move to the Jewish homeland Zionists had dreamed of. She knew it would be hard – the new nation had very little infrastructure and they would likely have to live in a makeshift camp for some time.

Béla did not share Magda's enthusiasm, and their friends and relatives thought the idea was crazy. 'At this time, with a baby and a toddler, you will go to Israel and live in a tent on the sand?' Some of Mum's family had already moved to Australia, and they encouraged her to go there first, then go to Israel when they had some money and it was more established. But Magda held firm.

'If everyone took this approach, of waiting for Israel to be established before moving there, where would Israel be?'

I imagine that in her mind, the conditions in Israel would never get close to anything she or Béla had endured during the war.

It's doubtful Béla or anyone else was going to stop Magda once she had this idea in her head. They packed all our belongings into a large wooden crate and we made our way to Marseille in France, then by boat to Haifa.

When we first arrived in Israel we were indeed living in a tent on the sand. There were thousands upon thousands of Holocaust survivors and their families fleeing Europe at this time. We then moved to a *ma'abarot*, which was a refugee camp where we lived in what looked like old airport hangars. There were thousands of refugees separated into family groups by curtains.

Béla had a brother, Dezsö, who had been living in what was then British-controlled Palestine since 1933. He had established himself as an engineer and Béla was able to work with him as a draftsman. Magda wanted to get a job in her profession as a kindergarten teacher. She approached the woman who was directing a kindergarten within the *ma'abarot*.

'Can you speak Hebrew?' the director asked.

'Just a few words,' said Magda.

'So how can you be a kindergarten teacher here?' scoffed the director.

'Trust me,' Magda said, 'there are children here from everywhere, all with different languages. If I show you that I can work with them will you give me the job?'

The director told Magda she would give her a chance. 'I'll leave you alone with the children for ten minutes. If you survive that time, you pass the test.'

Ten minutes later, Magda had children of at least forty different nationalities crawling all over her, laughing and giggling. She got the job.

This job was very important for Magda because it meant she could work and earn an income, and take Eva and me to work with her. She also had access to some European food, which was served at the kindergarten canteen. Much of the food served from the camp kitchens was more Middle Eastern in style, and it did not agree with Eva especially.

With so many people living so close together, hygiene was poor and illness was common. While the situation was nothing like what they had experienced in Auschwitz, it did make Magda nervous. And in any case, if she and Béla were going to build new lives in Israel, they needed to get out of this temporary situation as soon as they could.

A new housing development called Mivdeh Ezrachi was being established in Holon, not far from Tel Aviv, so Magda made enquiries about getting a house there. She found one, a very small two-room home, but it would cost money they didn't have. She was sharing this dilemma with a builder she'd met in the camp when he confided that he and his wife had fallen in love with Eva.

'My wife and I cannot have children. If you would allow us to adopt your youngest daughter, I will build you a house in return,' he said.

I was too young to remember this incident, but I imagine my mother thanking him with a laugh. Never in a million years would she have accepted such an offer. In the end, Magda swallowed her pride and begged Dezső to give them a loan, to which he agreed.

I have some memories of this time. I remember the small kindergarten my mother set up in the tiny garden at the back of our house. Magda would care for around a dozen children at a time, while my father worked with the city council. I remember that we saw a lot of Magda's friend from Auschwitz, Vera Fischer (now Vera Alexander) and her family, who lived only a short bus ride away in the packing shed of an orange orchard. Vera's husband, Stefan, was an artist who worked as a security guard at the orchard and had a studio in a pigeon coop. They had two boys who were about our age. I also remember having a 'boyfriend' when I was eight and a half. He was very jealous: he tied a piece of string between his wrist and mine, and if I talked to anyone for too long he would give me a yank to get me moving again.

Life in Mivdeh Ezrachi was quite free and comfortable. However, one of the conditions of living in Israel at that time was that all men aged forty-five years and under were required to devote one month each year to *miluim*, military service. Béla, forty at the time, had to do this, though he hated it. He was still scarred by the war, and he was no longer a young man so he found it very tiring – even more so because he had never been keen about moving to Israel in the first place.

———

For as long as we were in Israel, letters kept coming from family in Australia urging Magda and Béla to follow their lead and emigrate there. Almost all of the surviving Hellinger clan (in fact, most of the Slovak Jewish survivors of the Holocaust) had moved to Melbourne in 1948, and their letters spoke glowingly about how good life was in Australia.

'We understand your Zionism,' they would say, 'but enough already! You've done your bit. Come over here!'

For a time in the early fifties, Australia closed its borders to new arrivals, which gave Magda a convenient excuse for staying put. Then, in February 1956, visas for our entry to Australia arrived in the mail. Things were very different then – the family had been able to apply for visas on our behalf. Béla had turned forty-five and completed his final month of *miluim* the previous year. Finally, Magda conceded, and the decision was made to move to the other side of the world. I was nine and a half when we boarded an Air France flight with nothing more than a few suitcases.

For me and Eva it was a challenging time, as we had to leave without telling anyone. Mum had been insistent that we weren't to let any of our friends know what we were doing. She didn't want to be accused of being a traitor or a deserter. Then we landed in an English-speaking country when we didn't speak any English. Eva and I had spoken Czech until we learnt Hebrew, and now needed to change again. Of course, as with most young children, we adapted quite quickly. It was at this point that I started calling myself Maya, somehow thinking that it sounded more Western than Vera.

Melbourne was a long, long way from their pasts in almost every sense, but this time Magda and Béla found stability and opportunity. In booming post-war Australia, they once again set about building new lives for themselves and their daughters.

17

The legacy of tattoo 2318

Magda's experience of the war was never something that seemed to weigh on her. My sister and I weren't even conscious of either of our parents' status as Holocaust survivors until we were teenagers, but even then it didn't become a topic of family conversation. To us, and I think to all who knew them, they were a couple who arrived in Australia and set out on a mission to get on with their lives, to settle and establish themselves and to provide a good home for their children. Magda's way of coping was to look forward, not backwards, and to never see herself as a victim.

We arrived in Melbourne in 1956, and were soon embraced by the community of expatriate Slovakians, many of whom had come to Australia soon after the war, most in 1948. Mum was warmly welcomed at regular morning and afternoon teas with fellow Holocaust survivors, many of whom had been in the women's camps in Birkenau, including Camp C. As in any community, there were often family events as well, and we attended many of these.

There was just one lady, a cousin called Magda Englander, who used to badmouth Mum behind her back. She would complain about Mum to anyone who would listen. No one seemed to take her seriously, but after overhearing some of her comments one time, I asked Mum why she was speaking like this.

'How stupid Magda is,' Mum said. In her matter-of-fact way, she went on to tell me the story of how she'd saved Magda from Dr Klein during their time at Auschwitz–Birkenau by slapping her to make her see sense and understand that Klein's promised 'sanatorium' was a cruel trap.

'I saved her life, this time and other times, and all she remembers is the slap,' Mum said.

I would learn much later that accusations of collaboration had followed Mum, as they had many others who held functionary positions, for years – sometimes decades – after the war.

The first time my mother was accused was in Prague very soon after the war. Walking with Béla, she was on her way to meet her brother Ernest. A woman in the street recognised Magda and pointed her out to a nearby policeman. The policeman approached Magda and said, 'This woman accuses you of beating her up in a camp. You need to come with me now.'

At that moment, Ernest arrived at the scene. Having been a partisan, he was well connected and able to mention the names of a few prominent people he knew.

'I will vouch for her,' he told the policeman. 'I guarantee to bring her to the police station tomorrow. You cannot arrest her unless you have a specific crime to accuse her of.'

The next day, Magda went to the police station and stood in front of a magistrate. It turned out that the magistrate – his name was Korezina – had been in concentration camps himself so he had some understanding of what went on in these places.

'Tell me what happened,' he said to Magda's accuser.

The woman told of wanting to go on a cart during the death march, but Magda had pulled her off and slapped her face twice to stop her going.

'I know that she saved my life, but I don't forgive her for those slaps.'

Korezina listened patiently to the whole story.

Holding the accuser's gaze, he said, 'Aren't you ashamed to bring this woman in front of me? Do you not understand what Magda Hellinger did? How much she endangered her own life in front of the SS to prevent you going to your death? Shame on you. You should be thankful to her and apologise.'

At that, Magda said, 'I don't want anything from her. Let her go and that will be the end of this.'

Finally the judge looked at the accuser again and said, 'Shame on you. After all you both went through in the camps, now I have one Jewish woman accusing another. Disappear from my court. I don't want to see you again.'

He then said to Magda, 'I am proud of you.'

Magda received another request to attend a police station during another visit to Prague. This time the commander of the station was a Slovak who happened to know Magda. He told her there had been a complaint from a woman called Irena who, like the other person, had accused Mum of slapping her. This was Mum's cousin Irena, who Mum had also pulled off a cart. But there was no hearing this time. The commander told Magda that he knew her and understood that she wouldn't have done this for no reason. He had torn up the complaint, but wanted Magda to know about it.

The next time Mum was accused was in Israel, in the *ma'abarot*, the refugee camp. She was at the back of the camp doing her laundry amongst a number of others, me and my sister at her feet, when one of the women suddenly said, 'That's her! That's her! There she is!'

Soon all the women who had been doing their washing were pressing backwards away from Magda, and then they started screaming. Magda was left standing there with her two young children, not knowing what to do. Eventually she picked up her bundle of washing with one arm, picked up Eva with the other and pushed me in front to return to our tent.

Not long afterwards, Magda was told that a Hungarian woman had complained of her behaviour as *Lagerälteste* and that a magistrate would come from the town of Haifa to hear her accusations. In a makeshift courtroom, the situation played out in a similar way to what had happened in Prague. This time, the woman told the judge that Magda had slapped her twice while she was queuing up for soup.

When the judge asked Magda to respond, she said, 'I always tried to help, but sometimes I had to be strict if people weren't disciplined. I remember that in this situation, four women were carrying a large kettle of soup towards their barrack when this woman – my accuser – ran towards them, pushed through and tried to dip her bowl into the kettle out of turn. This caused the other women to drop the kettle. It splashed, spilling some of the precious soup and scalding the hands of two of the girls. I didn't want to slap anyone, but in this case I had to make an example. Can you imagine if a thousand women tried to push their way to the front? It would have been the sort of chaos that the SS loved to see, giving them an excuse to send the whole block to the gas chambers.'

The judge then asked the others in this 'courtroom' to speak up if they knew anything of this matter. An older woman raised her hand – she was perhaps fifty or so; older than Magda and the other women gathered there.

'I agree with Magda,' she said. 'Magda was like our mother. She was watching out for us. She was protecting us. And you want to accuse her?'

After this, the accuser withdrew her allegation and the judge dismissed the case.

There was one other situation a little later. That time it was a Tel Aviv judge who dismissed the case in a similar way.

Trials such as these were known as collaborator trials or honour trials. They took place all over Europe and in Israel, some highly formal and some less so.

Some were genuine attempts to punish Jews who had actively collaborated with the Germans for no reason other than to gain advantage for themselves. It's true that some functionaries took to their roles with excessive enthusiasm, and that some also took advantage of the situation for their own benefit.

But in many other cases, such as the ones Magda faced, accusations were an outlet for survivors to deal with what they had been through, and with what today would be recognised as survivor guilt and PTSD. Many Slovakian survivors were denounced and condemned based on hearsay, simply because they had managed to last so long in the camps. No doubt many of the 'ordinary' prisoners in Camp C – in this 'city' with a fluctuating population of up to 30,000 – saw someone like Magda running around, taking charge, sometimes threatening people with a stick – and interpreted such behaviour as a form of collaboration with the SS. They were in no position to understand the reality of the situation: that Magda and the other functionaries had no choice but to take on their appointed roles, and that if they did not maintain order or were deemed too 'soft', the SS would send them up the chimney without a second thought. And if they didn't maintain control in the camps, the SS would soon enforce it themselves.

The number of people tried in this fashion between 1945 and 1950 is unknown, but is thought to be in the low hundreds. Of these, only a small minority were found to be genuine collaborators.

———

On the evening of 27 June 2006, I returned from visiting my mother in the nursing home. Magda was eighty-nine years old, and since moving with her family to Australia fifty years earlier, she had lived a happy and, after years of hard work, comfortable life. She had lost her husband Béla only four years earlier, when he was ninety-two years old. It was so sad now to see her so frail.

I arrived home weighed down by sorrow. I sat down at my computer to answer some emails and, on an impulse, typed 'Magda Blau' into Google. There were various links to testimonies my mother had given over the years, to the Shoah Foundation, the United States Holocaust Memorial Museum (USHMM) and others, speaking of her wartime experiences. There were also links to other Magda Blaus. Amongst all these search results, one jumped out at me. The linked article had the heading: 'A Father's Memories of Auschwitz'. Under the main story was a sub-heading: 'Debra Fisher on Magda Blau, a survivor she never met'.

Scrolling down, I saw a photo of an arm tattooed with the numbers 2318. The photo was captioned: 'The concentration camp number of Magda Blau is tattooed on Debra Fisher's arm.'

I fell back in my chair.

What was going on here? Who was Debra Fisher? She wasn't someone Mum had ever mentioned. How did she know Mum? More importantly, why did she have Mum's number on her arm?

Unfortunately, Mum was not well enough for me to ask her anything about this. Her condition deteriorated quickly, and she died peacefully the next day.

In the Jewish tradition, the funeral was held on the following day, attended by my sister and me, our families and Mum's many friends. That evening, we hosted a minyan, a prayer service, at our home, and then my son Michael helped me track down a possible email address for Debra. I sent her a tentative enquiry and was stunned the next day when I received a lengthy email that started, 'Hello, my name is Debra Fisher.' As I read Debra's reply, I was comforted by the warmth I felt flowing from her words. She wrote with understanding, compassion and honesty, which was so helpful at such a sad and emotional time.

Debra told me she was a forty-seven-year-old occupational therapist from New York. She explained that her father, Oscar Fisher, a Hungarian, had been sent to Auschwitz towards the end of the war. He survived and lived on, though his parents, brother and three sisters were all murdered there. For many years, if Debra asked Oscar about his experience of Auschwitz, he painted a very benign picture. He told of playing tricks on the SS and stealing food without their realising it. It was only shortly before his death that Debra insisted he tell her the truth. His response was, 'If I let you in this room, you will never, ever get out.' Debra insisted that he let her in, and it was only then that he told her of the fear, pain, starvation and cruelty he had experienced. He was right: having entered it, Debra was unable to leave that room, and it was this that had motivated her in her quest to learn more and to educate others.

Oscar died at the relatively young age of sixty-three as a result of hepatitis he'd first contracted in Auschwitz. He was one of the many thousands who are not recorded as victims of the Holocaust but nevertheless had their lives cut short by their treatment at the hands of the Nazis.

After his death, Debra had wanted to honour her father in some way, but she couldn't work out how. Then, during a visit to the USHMM in Washington, she asked someone at the information desk to give her the testimony of a male survivor to listen to, along with one of a female survivor. The female recording they gave her was of Magda telling her story. At the end of the recording, Magda said, 'My name is 2318, that is how I was known for three-and-a-half years. Do not let the world forget.'

Magda's story, and especially that last line, struck a chord with Debra. In that moment she decided to have Magda's number tattooed onto her arm as a constant reminder of what her father and Magda had lived through. She hoped other people would ask about the tattoo, creating opportunities for her to share Magda's story.

I felt proud that my mother's story had affected Debra so much. Debra said she had made some efforts to contact Magda and seek her approval before she had the tattoo done. She had somehow tracked down Magda's address and written a couple of letters, but hadn't heard back. It's possible Mum assumed Debra was another academic seeking her account only to misconstrue it to fit some pre-determined story they intended to tell. In the end, Debra had decided to go ahead and get her arm tattooed, though she was still concerned that she hadn't been able to receive Magda's approval. I later reassured her that Mum would have been very proud, especially given Debra's purpose and sincerity.

Since receiving the tattoo, Debra had shared Magda's story in talks to various schools, churches and temples, as well as to countless strangers who had asked, 'What is that number on your arm?'

'Some people make a joke in order to broach the subject,' Debra wrote, 'such as whether it's part of my phone number or social security number. I never care. The bottom line is that they ask, and I can then tell them how your mother was a young girl taken from her family, how she shared her clothes with the peasant girls, how she convinced the stronger women to hold up the weakest ones in the roll calls, keeping them alive for another day. It is through stories like your mother's that we keep the memory of the Holocaust alive.'

Debra closed her letter by writing, 'The tattoo is nothing that I enjoy looking at, Maya. Some mornings when I shower I even wish it wasn't there. It is ugly, but I feel that wearing it and forcing these questions about the Holocaust from strangers and telling Magda Blau's story was the least I could do. I mean, what is it that a daughter of a Holocaust survivor should do, knowing that she grew up with "one of them", those incredible survivors?'

After those first emails, we were in touch constantly over the next few months, developing a strong friendship from opposite sides of the world.

———

I probably would never have discovered Debra Fisher if she hadn't shared her father's story at a StoryCorps recording booth at Grand Central Station. Her story was broadcast on NPR and featured on their website in 2005, then subsequently published in 2006 in a book called *Wisdom of Our Fathers*, collected by Tim Russert. This became the story I discovered through my internet search.

After I made contact with Debra, our joint story started to take on a life of its own.

A *New York Times* reporter contacted both of us and published a story in early November 2006. At the time my husband, Des, and I were planning a trip to Detroit, where we had some family, so I decided to add on a side trip to New York so I could meet Debra in person. I was invited to do an interview with Debra on NPR with Michele Norris on the 'All Things Considered' program.

I met Debra for the first time at the NPR studio on 24 November, just before we were due to do the interview. I liked her immediately. She was a genuine, positive person. Of course, the thing I wanted to see most was her tattoo, which was hidden under the long sleeves of her shirt. She was about to show it to me when she decided it would have more impact if she revealed it in the studio, while we were on air.

And so it was. Live in front of a radio audience of thousands, Debra pulled up her sleeve to show me the numbers on her arm. 2318.

'Oh,' I exclaimed. 'It's much neater than my mother's.'

Then I was overcome by emotions, and Debra took my hand.

'I can't believe it,' I said. I hadn't expected it to feel so scary, seeing those numbers on someone else's arm.

While I gathered myself, Debra explained to Michele that she'd felt scared getting the tattoo in the first place. She told of how, once she'd firmed in her decision, she'd gone into the first tattoo shop she came across in Norwalk, Connecticut and made her unusual request. The tattooist, a large, bearded man who looked like a motorcycle gang member, told her she was in the right place: he'd long had an interest in the Nazis and the Holocaust, including collecting memorabilia for a while. At that, Debra was ready to back out, but the tattooist assured her that he had long ago moved past any desire to emulate the Nazis, that he wanted to support her in her cause and that, thanks to his past interest in these things, he even knew what colour the ink needed to be.

By the time the interview came to an end, we were all crying, even Michele.

I was so glad to have met Debra, and we keep in touch to this day. The whole experience was so uncanny and incredible. But more than that, I was so encouraged by what she had done, by her courage in stepping forward and taking action to perpetuate the stories of the Holocaust. She gave life to my mother's memory in a way I never had. Mum had often talked about the camps, but my sister and I had only listened with one ear.

Meeting Debra gave me fresh impetus to tell this story – the story my mother always wanted to tell.

Epilogue

Magda never wanted thanks or praise from those whose lives she saved – just acknowledgement that she had done whatever she could in a truly horrific time, and that she had remained humane in the most inhumane of environments. Thankfully, in contrast to her accusers, there were many prisoners who recognised and were grateful for Magda's efforts.

Ilene Freier Brookler is a distant cousin who lives in Florida in the USA. While researching her own family's history, she met Magda and became immersed in her story and those of other *Blockältesten* in the women's camps. Ilene has done substantial research since, including interviewing Magda and many of these women in the 1990s. She has generously shared some of the comments made by her interviewees about their experiences with Magda.

> *In Birkenau I met Magda Hellinger from Michalovce. It was March, winter time. My shoes had been stolen and I was barefoot.*

*Magda brought me some shoes, which protected me against the
cold. She was also helpful in other situations and I feel deep
gratitude to her for saving my life.*

– Katarina Kollarova, number 26311,
who was deported from Hungary in 1944

*I knew Magda Hellinger and asked her to look after my mother,
and she did. She took her to a block where Marika Klein was the*
Blockälteste *and told her to look after my mother. During selections
Marika made sure my mother was inside or in the kitchen, so my
mother was never selected. Magda also visited my mother often. One
day she found my mother could not talk and asked her what was
wrong. My mother pointed to her throat. Her tonsils were swollen. If
the SS saw that she would be sent to the gas chambers immediately.
Magda arranged for a prisoner doctor to see her and remove her
tonsils using a sterilised knife. This saved my mother's life.*

– Helen Gottlieb, number 5968, came to Camp C
in Birkenau with her mother

*Magda entered the barrack with the Germans and recognised
me, her cousin from Michalovce. I don't know how she recognised
me because I did not recognise myself. She said to me, "What are
you doing on this Hungarian transport?" She told me to come to
her barrack at night and she will give me food. She also told me
selections are bad and not to trust the Germans. When I asked
her how to get out of Auschwitz, she pointed to the chimneys.
She helped me as much as she could. She could not save everybody,
but she helped a lot of people. Magda arranged for me to be in
charge of the Hofcommando (cleaning group). Together with*

100 other girls, we had to clean the barracks and thus avoided
many selections because we were inside the barracks at that time . . .
The Germans needed the Jews to do their dirty work. Magda's job
was a very hard one, no one realises how stressful it was to keep
30,000 girls in order. I am grateful to her for going out of her way
to help, particularly when we hardly knew each other.

– Elsa Krauss, who arrived at Birkenau in March 1944
from Hungary. She was not tattooed.

Over the years, others have told me their stories, or the stories of
their parents, and their interactions with Magda in the camps.
(These stories have been lightly edited for clarity.)

My mother, Ruzena Neumann, was lucky in that hell of a place
to be with her mother, Perle, an aunt, Rivka, and two cousins,
Esther and Montzi. One of the main contributing factors to their
survival of Auschwitz was that they were occasionally able to have
access to some extra food. After I moved to Melbourne, we used to
drive past a shoe shop on Toorak Road. My mother told me that the
owner of that shop was Eva, the daughter of Magda Hellinger, who
had been Lagerälteste *in their camp at Birkenau. She told me it*
was Magda who had organised this food for Perle, who was then
able to share it with not only my mother but also the other two
cousins and other nieces who would visit her from other barracks.
The other factor in their survival was that Magda organised
them to be transferred to work in the Krupp munitions factory
in Silesia, Poland. This factory provided better conditions, e.g.
beds with proper bedding, warmer clothing and the guards who
were more humane. Sometimes my mother even got to work in the

*kitchen, which was an opportunity to obtain more food. After my
mother got a splinter while assembling the grenades, she developed
a temperature and was allowed a day off! Another very important
point was that the factory did not force its inmates on the death
marches. In the end the whole family survived except poor Montzi,
who suffered from tuberculosis before the war and died not long
after arriving at the factory.*

— Helen Goston, daughter of Ruzena Neumann,
who survived the war

When I heard that the Lagerälteste's *name was Hellinger and
that she was from Michalovce, I wondered if we might be cousins.
We had Hellingers in our family who lived in the same town.
I approached her and we discovered that we were in fact cousins.
Magda found work for me and my sister Lili in the kitchen, which
kept us away from roll calls and selections. Later, Magda was
able to arrange "good" transports because she was a big shot. She
arranged for me, Lili and two of our cousins to go to the Siemens
factory in Nuremberg, which saved our lives.*

— Yolli Frank, number 41663

Magda was resilient, courageous, fearless and daring. She was
always hopeful and optimistic. These were the qualities that
helped her survive the atrocities of Auschwitz–Birkenau and save
the lives of countless others. She never saw herself as a saviour
nor as being on a mission. She was simply someone who saw
opportunities and had the fortitude to navigate the conflicting
emotions of fear and hope – and to help others do the same.
These qualities also helped her after the war.

Magda was not one to talk often of her experiences of the war. She was certainly not someone who regarded herself as a victim or held grudges. She did not speak of her feelings about the war or of her desire that the truth of the war be told. It was only through her formal testimonies and her writing that she discussed the lasting impact the war had on most survivors. I will give her the last word here, drawing on statements she made at the end of many of her testimonies.

For those who survived the misery, there were marks on their lives. Many had terrible dreams for the rest of their lives. After they came back, there wasn't anyone who could understand them, so survivors looked to other survivors for support. Many died young. There was a woman who worked in Kanada, the storage room for all the belongings of the new arrivals. She often smuggled clothing to the camp under her dress to give to friends who needed it badly. She knew that if the SS found out what she was doing she would pay for it with her life. Sometimes she also smuggled food from other storerooms. We visited her and her husband after the war and she told us that she couldn't sleep at night because she had ongoing nightmares. Instead she worked, cleaning, cooking and baking at night. One day we went to see her for lunch and found her sitting with her eyes more closed than open. She was hardly able to eat anything. This beautiful, courageous woman was fading away.

There are people, some writers, professors, scientists, who for unbelievable reasons try to deny that the Holocaust took place. They try to say the Holocaust was a hoax. Others say it happened a long time ago and that it should be forgotten.

Unfortunately, all the barbarism of the German SS, the sadism, the deception, the cruelty, was true, and its impact continues. We saw our friends, lovely young girls, becoming wilted flowers. We would see a drunk SS guard brutally beat or kick a young woman and we could do nothing to help. Even feeling anger or sadness didn't help, so we suppressed these feelings. There aren't any survivors who are not haunted to some degree by memories of the cruelty, the sickness, the destitution.

So I turn to you, parents, teachers, professors, scientists, preachers, priests, rabbis. Educate the children and the general public about those horrors perpetrated on all nations, not only Jews, under the Nazi regime. I witnessing myself that nobody was exempt. We must make the wrong right. Be understanding and helpful to the remaining survivors. It's not right to avoid talking about it for shame or frustration. Don't minimise the Holocaust as an old story, so that tragedies like it never have the chance to happen again . . . ever.

Notes on the post-war fates of prominent people in this story

Katja Singer was transferred from Auschwitz–Birkenau to the Stutthof concentration camp in 1944 after being accused by the SS of helping inmates to survive. She survived the remainder of the war only because the gas chamber at Stutthof was out of order. She married, had children, became an art gallery curator for the Czech government, and lived out her life in Prague. Magda was in regular contact with Katja and visited her a number of times. Other than giving a single interview to the *Jewish Currents* magazine in 2011, Katja recorded no testimonies of her time in the camps.

Magda also kept in touch with Vera Alexander (*née* Fischer) and her family for many years. They continued to live in Israel. Vera gave testimony at the trial of Adolf Eichmann in 1961.

Magda's older brother Max, who had originally moved to Palestine in 1933, settled in Australia in 1951. Ernest moved to Israel after the war and then to Australia in 1961, while

Eugene emigrated to the USA, where he lived in Hawaii and then San Diego.

Cousins Irena and Piri, who were on the death march with Magda, both lived out their lives in Israel. Magda Englander emigrated to Australia, the *Läuferin* Aliska moved to Israel and then Australia, and Magda's other cousin Lili emigrated to Canada. Edith, with whom Magda had cracked lice in the early days of Birkenau, settled in Australia. She and Magda met each other by chance one day in 1958 and they remained friends. Zsuzsi Tisza and her mother emigrated to Melbourne, Australia, where Zsuzsi still lives today.

Magda maintained contact with many of these women; she never held a grudge against those such as Irena or Magda Englander who accused her of treachery or collaboration.

Erich Kulka returned to Prague and then moved to Israel. He wrote many books about the Holocaust and Auschwitz, and he and Magda exchanged many letters as she contributed to his research.

As Marta had flagged after Magda's return to Michalovce, she and her family emigrated to Argentina soon after the end of the war. She and Magda remained in regular contact, and Marta visited Australia in 1971 to attend my sister Eva's wedding.

After the premature death of Ruzenka Hellinger in 1946, Béla Hellinger emigrated to Israel, where he later remarried.

My father's sister Aranka, her husband Jancsi and their son Tommy also moved to Israel. Aranka unfortunately died quite young, but Jancsi lived into his nineties. Tommy still lives in Israel with his wife Nitzi, children Ram and Iris, and his grandchildren.

———

Notes on the post-war fates of prominent people in this story

Magda had no contact with Dr Gisella Perl after the war until 1953 when, while we were still living in Israel, Mum noticed a newspaper advertisement for a public talk Gisella was to give to Romanian expatriates. Magda and Béla went to the venue, arriving after Gisella had started speaking. She noticed my parents at the back of the room, interrupted herself, left the podium and rushed to give Magda a hug. They spoke for just a few moments before Gisella continued her presentation. Magda and Béla returned home and Magda wrote a brief letter to Gisella. In response, Gisella wrote an open letter to the *Új-Kelet* Hungarian-language newspaper, from which an extract is featured in the introduction to this book. Dr Perl became a prominent gynaecologist and infertility specialist in Israel. She and Mum remained in constant contact until Gisella died in 1988 at the age of eighty-one.

Dr Adélaïde Hautval was the other prisoner-doctor with whom Magda had significant dealings and who survived the war. Magda was reminded of Adélaïde while travelling in Israel some years later. She and Béla visited an avenue of honour in front of the Yad Vashem World Holocaust Remembrance Center, where they found a tree honouring Dr Hautval. She had been named 'Righteous Among the Nations' in 1965, an honour bestowed by the nation of Israel on non-Jews who risked their lives during the Holocaust to save Jews from execution. Magda sent Adélaïde a photo of herself under this tree. She and Magda stayed in contact until Adélaïde died in 1988, aged eighty-two.

Most, though not all, of the more prominent Nazis who knew Magda's name were captured and tried for war crimes in the years after the war. Irma Grese and Josef Kramer were tried in the Belsen trial and executed in 1945. Johann Schwarzhuber never made it to Switzerland. He was captured at Ravensbrück, tried and executed for war crimes in 1947. Eduard Wirths was captured by British forces and hanged himself in 1945 while in custody. Margot Drechsler was captured and executed by the Russians in May 1945, while Maria Mandel was executed after the Auschwitz trials in 1948. Luise Danz also faced that trial, but escaped with a life sentence. She was subsequently released in 1956 and lived on to the age of ninety-one. Josef Mengele escaped to Argentina, where he lived until dying of a stroke in 1979.

Glossary

Aufseherin: title given to ordinary female SS guards. Female SS guards at all levels were collectively known as SS-Helferin, or female SS helpers.

Blockälteste/Blockältesten (pl.): block eldest; block leader. A prisoner functionary responsible for day-to-day organisation of an accommodation block, including hygiene and food distribution. In the women's camps at Auschwitz–Birkenau, most were Jewish inmates.

Blockführer: SS guard in charge of an accommodation block.

Brotkammer: 'bread room', or bakery.

Effektenlager: known as 'Kanada'. The warehouse that stored goods confiscated from prisoners on arrival.

Entwesungsanlage: disinfection facility known as 'sauna'. Facility used for processing new arrivals, including hair removal and delousing.

Hashomer Hatzair: Jewish Zionist youth organisation.

SS-Hauptsturmführer: captain (SS rank).

Kapo: prisoner in charge of a Kommando. These were often German criminals.

Kommando: outdoor working group.

Lagerälteste/Lagerältesten (pl.): camp eldest; camp leader. A prisoner functionary responsible for day-to-day operation of an entire camp or camp sector.

Lagerführer (m), Lagerführerin (f): SS guard in charge of a camp or camp sector. The full titles were *Schutzlagerführer* and *Schutzlagerführerin*

Lagerkommandant: camp commander. Most senior member of a concentration camp administration.

Läuferinnen (f) (pl.): runner, often a younger person who would run errands and carry messages for a prisoner functionary.

SS-Obersturmführer: SS rank. Junior to *Hauptsturmführer*.

Politische Abteilung: 'Political department' – internal camp intelligence, operated as an arm of the Gestapo, or Nazi secret police.

Glossary

Prisoner functionary: generic term for any prisoner carrying out leadership or other official duties in a concentration camp at the behest of the SS.

Rapportschreiberin (f): a prisoner functionary who officially acted as record keeper, but who also performed an organisational role in the appointment of other prisoner functionaries within the camps.

Revier: camp word for infirmary/camp hospital (German word for sick bay).

Schutzhaftlagerführer: senior operational SS position within a concentration camp.

Stabsgebäude: main office (and accommodation for office staff).

Stubenälteste/Stubenältesten (pl.): room 'eldest'; second in charge to a *Blockälteste*, sometimes in charge of a single room in larger blocks.

Stubendienst/Stubendienster (pl.): room helper, or room assistant. Subordinate to the *Blockälteste* and *Stubenälteste*.

Zählappell/Zählappelle (pl.): roll call. Sometimes shortened to Appell.

The Auschwitz complex consisted of three main concentration camps: Auschwitz I, Auschwitz II–Birkenau (often referred to as

277

just Birkenau) and Auschwitz III–Monowitz. In addition, over thirty smaller sub-camps were administered as part of Auschwitz.

The Birkenau camp included a number of self-contained 'sectors', designated as sectors B-Ia, B-Ib, B-IIa, etc. Of these, some became known simply by their suffix, so sector B-IIc was known as C Lager, or Camp C; and B-IId as D Lager, or Camp D.

Acknowledgements

When searching for a writer to help me expand my mother's memoir, I could not have imagined how lucky I was that David Brewster was available for this incredible project. We have enjoyed a strong and respectful creative partnership and I thank him so much for helping me to fulfil my mother's wish to have her story told. His amazing writing talent was instrumental in having the story recognised by the Simon & Schuster publishers.

Ilene Freier Brookler has been researching the *Blockältesten* of Auschwitz–Birkenau for many years and has interviewed many of them. She generously provided an enormous amount of background material including transcripts and recordings of interviews she conducted with Magda and other Auschwitz survivors.

It was Michelle Swainson at Simon & Schuster Australia who first recognised the potential of this story. She and Fiona Henderson have shepherded me through the process from start to finish and have provided enormous support.

My family, including my daughter Jenni Lee, son Michael Lee, granddaughters Arianne Matthaei Fink and Alexi Fink, sister Eva Demsky and her husband David, have provided encouragement and support all the way through. My great-niece Ellie Robinson has also shown keen interest. My late husband, Des Lee – a Holocaust survivor himself – is sadly not here to see the finished product.

Throughout this journey, I have greatly appreciated the ongoing support and encouragement of Judy Fischer, Rosie Lew, Cathie Kennedy, Barbara Sacks and Julie Butcher. Thanks too to all my friends, too many to mention, who have closely followed the progress of this book and been excited to hear every detail.

Finally, the gentleman from Perth who unwittingly provided the impetus for writing this book after pointing out an omission from Magda's original publication, and Debra Fisher, who also unknowingly, provided further inspiration when she chose to tattoo Magda's concentration camp number onto her arm.

Maya Lee

About the authors

Magda Hellinger was deported to Auschwitz on the second transport from Slovakia in March 1942, at the age of twenty-five. She was one of the very few to survive over three years in concentration camps. During her time in Auschwitz-Birkenau she held various prisoner functionary positions and had direct dealings with prominent SS personnel, using her unique position to save hundreds of lives.

Maya Lee is the daughter of Magda Hellinger. She is an accomplished businesswoman and fundraiser with several non-profit organisations. After co-authoring an autobiography of her Holocaust-survivor husband, Des Lee, Maya conducted wide-ranging research to fill out her mother's story and *The Nazis Knew My Name* is the result.

David Brewster is a Melbourne-based freelance writer whose work is centred on helping memoirists tell their stories. David's published works include *Scattered Pearls*, co-written with Sohila Zanjani, and *Around the Grounds*, co-written with Peter Newlinds.